MOViE CLiPS For Kids

The Sequel

Group
Loveland, Colorado

Group resources actually work!

This Group resource helps you focus on **"The 1 Thing™"**— a life-changing relationship with Jesus Christ. "The 1 Thing" incorporates our **R.E.A.L.** approach to ministry. It reinforces a growing friendship with Jesus, encourages long-term learning, and results in life transformation, because it's:

Relational
Learner-to-learner interaction enhances learning and builds Christian friendships.

Experiential
What learners experience through discussion and action sticks with them up to 9 times longer than what they simply hear or read.

Applicable
The aim of Christian education is to equip learners to be both hearers and doers of God's Word.

Learner-based
Learners understand and retain more when the learning process takes into consideration how they learn best.

Visit our Web site: **www.grouppublishing.com**

Credits
Contributing Authors: Ruthie Daniels, Laure Herlinger, Keith D. Johnson, Jan Kershner, Julie Lavender, Julie Meikeljohn, Jennifer Nystrom, Christopher Perciante, Donna Simcoe, Gary W. Troutman, and Helen Turnbull
Editors: Mikal Keefer and Amy Nappa
Chief Creative Officer: Joani Schultz
Copy Editor: Christy Fagerlin
Art Director: Sharon Anderson
Designer: Susan Tripp
Cover Art Director: Jeff A. Storm
Cover Designer: Alan Furst Inc.
Cover Illustrator: Patty O'Friel
Production Manager: Peggy Naylor

Unless otherwise noted, Scripture taken from the HOLY BIBLE, NEW INTERNATIONAL VERSION®. Copyright © 1973, 1978, 1984 by International Bible Society. Used by permission of Zondervan Publishing House. All rights reserved.

Library of Congress Cataloging-in-Publication Data
Movie clips for kids : the sequel.
      p. cm.
      ISBN 0-7644-2692-3 (pbk.)
      1. Motion pictures in Christian education. I. Group Publishing.
      BV1535.4.M69 2004
      268'.67–dc22   2003026548

10 9 8 7 6 5 4 3 2 1   13 12 11 10 09 08 07 06 05 04

Printed in the United States of America.

CONTENTS

Old Testament Devotions

New Testament Devotions

Hot Topics

LIGHTS! CAMERAS! ACTION!

Children of all ages love the movies! Have you ever noticed how turning on the television or popping in a video immediately captures the attention of children? And kids remember what they see on the screen. Ask them about a recent trip to the movie theater, and kids will be able to tell you about the plot, their favorite characters, and many will even quote lines that made them laugh.

What a great teaching tool we have! Since movies captivate their audiences, why not use them to help that audience learn about Jesus? *Movie Clips for Kids—The Sequel* offers one hundred clips you can use to teach over eighty Bible stories or themes to your kids. And every clip offers an exciting, active-learning experience. That way, you don't have to go from a captivating clip to a boring lecture. Instead, you can weave the movie clip into a fun activity that reinforces your Bible lesson.

There are several ways you can use this book. In the Table of Contents you'll find a listing of devotions for Old Testament accounts, New Testament accounts, and a listing of Hot Topics. There's a separate topical index at the end of the book that lists additional topics for which you can use the movie clips and another index that lists the movies by title. Then you can grab your movie, and you're ready to go!

A Few Important Details

In general, federal copyright laws do not allow you to use videos or DVDs (even ones you own) for any purpose other than home viewing. Though some exceptions allow for the use of short segments of copyrighted material for educational purposes, it's best to be on the safe side. Your church can obtain a license from the Motion Picture Licensing Corporation for a small fee. Just visit www.mplc.com or call 1-800-462-8855 for more information. When using a movie that is not covered by the license, we recommend directly contacting the movie studio to seek permission for use of the clip.

WARNING! We've also asked our authors to work hard to keep the movie segments wholesome and appropriate for children's ministry. You'll notice that all of the clips are rated G or PG. But that doesn't guarantee that you or someone in your church won't find the clip offensive. **Make sure you watch the clip before you show it to the children in your ministry.**

You'll also have to remember that children may see your showing of the clip as an endorsement of the whole movie. While the clip may be perfectly innocent, a child may go home excitedly and say, "Guess what we watched at church today?" The parents may watch the movie and call you the next day saying, "I can't believe you let my child watch that movie! Our pastor is going to hear about this!" The parent may be overreacting, or the parent may have a good point. Either way, parents have a right to protect their children. So you may want to let parents know that you're planning on using movie clips and how you'll use them. Just because you think the movie is OK doesn't mean every parent will. We've included a photocopiable letter and movie announcement on pages 7 and 8 that you can use to communicate with parents. You can photocopy the pages and send them out or adjust them to meet your needs.

Finding the Clips

To make it easier for you, we've provided approximate times for when each clip begins along with cues, such as a line of dialogue, or what's happening on the screen. Many videos include previews for other features and additional advertisements, and this can affect the start time for your movie clip. To make the start times more accurate, start the timing display feature on your player at the point where the production company's logo screen appears. For example, begin when the lion roars on an MGM movie or when the white castle appears on a blue screen for a Disney movie.

For movies that have been remade or have several versions, we've added the year of the version we used.

Allergy Alert

Whenever food is used in this book, you'll see this symbol.

Be aware that some children have food allergies that can be dangerous. Know your children, and consult with parents about allergies their children may have. Also be sure to carefully read food labels, as hidden ingredients may cause allergy-related problems.

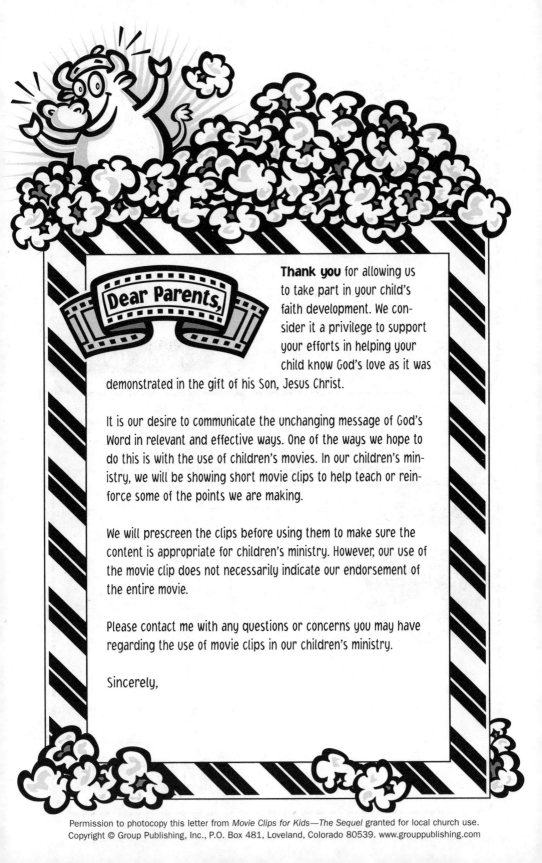

Dear Parents,

Thank you for allowing us to take part in your child's faith development. We consider it a privilege to support your efforts in helping your child know God's love as it was demonstrated in the gift of his Son, Jesus Christ.

It is our desire to communicate the unchanging message of God's Word in relevant and effective ways. One of the ways we hope to do this is with the use of children's movies. In our children's ministry, we will be showing short movie clips to help teach or reinforce some of the points we are making.

We will prescreen the clips before using them to make sure the content is appropriate for children's ministry. However, our use of the movie clip does not necessarily indicate our endorsement of the entire movie.

Please contact me with any questions or concerns you may have regarding the use of movie clips in our children's ministry.

Sincerely,

On _____,

our children's ministry will show a short clip

from the movie _____

_____

as a tool to teach children about _____

_____

_____

_____.

Please let us know if you have
any questions or concerns.

Thank you!

On _____,

our children's ministry will show a short clip

from the movie _____

_____

as a tool to teach children about _____

_____

_____

_____.

Please let us know if you have
any questions or concerns.

Thank you!

CREATION

Scripture: Genesis 1:1–2:3

Movie Title:
ATLANTIS: THE LOST EMPIRE (PG)

The Critics Say

You can also use this clip to teach children about the historical accuracy of the Bible and that we have a written account of how our world was created.

Start Time: 54 minutes, 5 seconds

Where to Begin: Kida and Milo are talking about Atlantis as they are chasing fireflies, and Milo is expressing interest in finding out more about Atlantis' history.

Where to End: Milo and Kida come up out of the water, and Milo exclaims, "It's amazing! A complete history of Atlantis!"

Plot: Milo and Kida are trying to find the secret of Atlantis. Milo wants to find out more about Atlantis' history, so Kida takes him to an underwater location where they find unknown writings. Milo deciphers these as the complete history of Atlantis.

Review: You can use this scene to help the children understand that God has given us the book of Genesis as a complete history of how our earth began and how humans were created. In understanding that God is the creator of everything, we can begin to get a glimpse of his greatness.

The Critics Say

In the world of Atlantis, they worshipped many false gods. Make sure you emphasize the point that there is only one true God, the God that created our universe.

Supplies: Bible, newsprint, 9x12 sheets of construction paper, 8 1/2 x11 sheets of white paper, hole punches, markers, and 12-inch lengths of ribbon

Preshow: Write "A History of Me" on newsprint, and post it on the wall.

NOW PLAYING

Place markers, hole punches, and ribbon where children can reach them. Give each child a 9x12 piece of construction paper, two pieces of white paper, and a 12-inch piece of ribbon. Have children fold their pieces of paper in half to form a booklet with the construction paper as a cover, then punch two holes along the binding side of the booklet about two inches apart. Thread the ribbon through the holes, and tie in a bow to bind the book together. On the outside have kids write the words "A History of Me." On the first page, they can draw a picture of themselves and write their names. On the next page, they can draw or write about their families. Then have each child draw a picture of the place he or she was born. The rest of the book is for kids to fill out as they please. Older children can tell about their school; younger children can draw pictures of their favorite things.

Say→ We're going to watch a scene from *Atlantis: The Lost Empire*. Milo and Kida are about to discover some secrets about Atlantis. Let's watch.

Show the *Atlantis: The Lost Empire* clip.

Ask→ • How do you think Milo felt when he found the writings?

• How would you feel if you found something like that that told about the beginnings of our world?

Say→ Did you know that we already have a complete history of how our world began? It's right here in the Bible!

Hold up your Bible.

Say→ We can read how God created *everything* from absolutely *nothing*. We can also read how he created us.

We can read the complete history of how we began anytime we want by just opening our Bibles. We don't have to decipher any strange writings or dig up any fossils. God created all of us and loves us very much because we are his creation.

Ask→ • How do you feel when you make something that turns out as good or better than you planned?

• How do you think God feels when he looks at his creation?

• How do you feel about the One who created you?

CAIN AND ABEL

Scripture: Genesis 4:1-15

 Movie Title:
THE PARENT TRAP (1961) (G)

You could use this movie clip to teach children about anger management or getting along with family members.

Start Time: 13 minutes

Where to Begin: One of the twin sisters slaps the other, and a fight begins.

Where to End: After they stop fighting, and the counselor says, "Let the punishment fit the crime."

Plot: Identical twins, separated since early childhood, are reunited at summer camp. They form a plan to switch identities in an effort to get their divorced parents back together.

Review: You can use this scene to introduce the concept of not only sibling rivalry, but downright sibling animosity. Watching the sisters argue will provide a natural tie-in to the story of Cain and Abel, with its jealousy, anger, and much uglier outcome than the siblings experience in the movie.

Supplies: Bible and Wint-o-Green Life Savers. Allergy **ALERT**

now PLAYING

Say→ We're going to watch a scene from an old movie called *The Parent Trap*. In this scene identical twins, separated since they were babies, meet again at summer camp. Let's see what happens at what *should* be a happy reunion!

Show the clip from *The Parent Trap*.

Ask→ • How did the sisters react to each other?

• Have you ever been in a situation where you didn't get along with someone? Tell a partner about it without using names.

Say→ When two people don't get along, the sparks can really fly. That's what happened to the sisters in the movie. Let's do a little experiment that might send some sparks flying.

Give each child a Wint-o-Green Life Savers candy, but tell kids not to eat the candy just yet. Turn off the lights in your room, pull down the shades, and otherwise make the room as dark as possible. Demonstrate how to bite down on a candy with your teeth. In doing so, you'll create small sparks that will be visible in the dark.

Have kids form pairs, and let partners take turns making sparks with their candy. (Have extra candy on hand so kids can try more than once.) Then turn on the lights, and let kids stay in their pairs.

Say→ The Bible tells about two brothers who *really* didn't get along!

Have kids read Genesis 4:1-15, or briefly tell the story in your own words. Then have partners answer the following questions.

Ask→ • Why did sparks fly between Cain and Abel?

• How could Cain have handled the situation differently?

• What do you think of God's punishment of Cain?

Say→ Cain sure did the wrong thing with his anger. We all get mad sometimes, but violence isn't the answer. When you're angry, it's a perfect time to turn to God. God will always help us resolve our conflicts.

In the movie clip we watched, the sisters were punished for their fighting. In the Bible, Cain was punished too. God could have destroyed Cain, but he didn't. Even when he has to punish us, God still demonstrates his love.

Give kids each a candy to take home to remind them to turn to God when they're angry rather than letting the sparks fly!

THE FLOOD (1)

Scripture: Genesis 6:9–8:22

Movie Title:
LILO & STITCH (PG)

Use this clip to teach about family.

The Critics Say

Scene 1 Start Time: 35 minutes, 25 seconds

Where to Begin: Lilo and Noni walk into their house and flip on the lights. Lilo says, "You'll like it a lot."

Where to End: An exhausted and frustrated Noni collapses on the couch.

Scene 2 Start Time: 1 hour, 6 minutes.

Where to Begin: Noni is crying and kneeling on the ground.

Where to End: Noni, Stitch, and the two aliens ride off on the motorcycle to rescue Lilo.

Plot: Two Hawaiian girls and their dangerous alien "puppy," Stitch, discover the true meaning of the Hawaiian word for family, *ohana*.

Review: Use these scenes to help children understand that God will never leave behind or forget those who believe in him.

Supplies: Slips of paper, pen, and envelope

Preshow: Write the following role descriptions on slips of paper, and put the slips in the envelope.

- **Leader:** Lead the group into another room, and line them up by height.

- **Encourager:** Encourage everyone to do what the leader says.

- **Tourist:** Pretend you don't understand the language the others in your class are speaking.

- **Disabled Person:** Pretend to have a disability that might make it difficult to follow directions and communicate.

The Critics Say

If you have fewer than five students, use the leader role, the encourager role, and at least one of the remaining roles. If you have more than five students, you can double any of the roles except the leader.

now PLAYING

Say→ In these scenes from *Lilo & Stitch*, we'll see how Lilo, Noni, and Stitch come to understand the true meaning of *ohana*, or *family*.

Play the first clip. While you are fast-forwarding to the second clip,

Ask→ • How would you feel if you were Lilo? if you were Noni? if you were Stitch?

Play the second clip.

Ask→ • Why do you think Stitch felt it was important to not leave anyone behind?

Say→ In the story of the Great Flood, God made the decision to flood the world to rid it of evil. Noah and his family were part of God's *ohana,* or *family.* He guided Noah and his family to safety. Now we're going to experience an activity in which you will be guided to "safety."

Explain that you're going to pass around an envelope with slips of paper in it. Each slip has special instructions; students shouldn't reveal what their slips say. Explain that kids will have a task to complete. Begin the activity tasks when each person has received a slip. After the activity is completed,

Ask→ • Do you think it was easy or difficult to make sure nobody was left behind in this activity? Explain.

Say→ Stitch learned the true meaning of family. He realized that he was an important part of the family, and he couldn't leave anyone behind. God didn't leave Noah behind, and God also won't leave us behind. We can always trust that because we are treasured members of God's *ohana,* we will always be safe and protected.

THE FLOOD (2)

Scripture: Genesis 6:9–8:22

 Movie Title:
THE RESCUERS DOWN UNDER (G)

The Critics Say

This clip can also be used to discuss the penalty of sin and obedience to God.

Start Time: 1 hour, 8 minutes

Where to Begin: McCleach fires his gun at the rope that's holding young Cody above an alligator-infested river.

Where to End: Cody is saved and reaches behind him to reveal Bernard hanging onto the broken rope.

Plot: McCleach, an evil poacher, will stop at nothing to capture wild animals. He's also captured and imprisoned a young Australian boy, Cody, who was attempting to free McCleach's captives. McCleach deliberately sends Cody to an assured death in an alligator-infested river. With the help of two mice, Marahute, the eagle, is freed and in turn, saves Cody's life.

Review: Use this clip to help children understand God's provision. Noah was a good man surrounded by corrupt and evil people. God took care of Noah and his family. God also saved all the animals of creation from the terrible flood. In this movie Marahute took care of Cody and saved his life similarly to God's provision of us.

Supplies: Stuffed animals, pillows, and masking tape

Preshow: Use masking tape to mark a river on the floor. Indicate a starting point and a finishing point.

NOW PLAYING

Say→ The Bible tells us that God helped Noah take care of all the animals of creation and saved them from the flood. Let's play a relay game and rescue some animals.

Have children form pairs and line up beside the river. Show the first pair of children how to grasp onto the elbows of their partners, facing one another. Have another child lay the pillow on top of his or her arms and place a stuffed animal on the pillow.

Say→ Let's pretend the pillow is our boat, and we have to get the animals to the other side of the raging river. On "Go," you and your partner will run to the other side, leave the stuffed animal, then return the boat to the next pair. That pair will then do the same thing with the next animal. Let's see how long it takes to get all the animals to the other side of the river.

Start the game, and encourage everyone to cheer as they move the animals to the other side.

The Critics Say

If you don't have enough stuffed animals for this game, begin the activity by having each child draw an animal that was on the ark. Encourage each person on a team to draw something different. Use the drawings for the game.

Say→ We saved the animals! The Bible tells us that God took care of Noah and his family too. He saved Noah, his family, and all of the animals from the flood. Let's watch a scene from *The Rescuers Down Under* to see who takes care of a boy named Cody.

Show the *Rescuers Down Under* clip.

Ask→ • Who rescued Cody and Bernard from the water?

• How is that like Noah, his family, and the animals being rescued from the flood?

• How does God rescue us and save us from death?

Say→ God saved Noah and all of his family. God takes care of us, too. In the movie, the eagle saves Cody and Bernard from drowning. God sent his son, Jesus, to save us from death, so that we may have eternal life.

TOWER OF BABEL (1)

Scripture: Genesis 11:1-8

Movie Title:
THE LION KING (G)

You can also use this clip to teach about greed for power or making bad choices.

Start Time: 26 minutes, 50 seconds

Where to Begin: Scar says, "Precisely" and begins to sing "Be Prepared."

Where to End: At the end of Scar's song.

Plot: The evil Scar, King Mufasa's brother, plots to overthrow Mufasa, kill Simba, and take over the kingdom.

Review: Use this scene to help children understand that God's power is the ultimate power and that we can trust God's power instead of trying to grab power for ourselves.

Supplies: Newsprint, tape, and marker

Preshow: Tape the newsprint on the wall.

NOW PLAYING

Write "Power" at the top of the newsprint.

Say→ **Let's think of powerful people we know or have heard of. Let's first think of people who have powerful bodies.**

Write the names as children call them out. Kids might include professions such as wrestler, athlete, or fire fighter, or they might call out the names of people in professions such as these.

Say→ **People with a lot of money are often considered powerful, too. Let's think of people who have this kind of power.**

Continue to brainstorm with children, including people who are powerful because they're intelligent, because they're popular, and because they have a position of authority. After you've got a long list,

Ask→ • **How do you think God might feel about human power?**

• **When is the power of these people worthless? What are things they can't do, even with the power they have?**

Say→ **We're going to watch a scene from *The Lion King*. In this scene, we'll see the evil Scar plotting to use his power to take over the kingdom.**

Play the clip.

Ask→ • **Why do you think Scar is plotting to take over the kingdom?**

• **What kind of power does Scar have?**

• **How will he use this power?**

• **Do you think actions like these would please God?**

Say→ In the story of the Tower of Babel, people decided to build a tower to heaven to reach God. While they were attempting this, they forgot that they needed to trust in God's power rather than try to grab power for themselves. God was not pleased with the actions and attitudes of the people building the tower. He wanted them to remember his power.

We may try in our lives to be powerful in various ways, but the only *true* power belongs to God, and he wants us to trust him rather than try to gain power for ourselves.

TOWER OF BABEL (2)

Scripture: Genesis 11:1-8

Movie Title:
THE EMPEROR'S NEW GROOVE (G)

The Critics Say
You can also use this scene to talk about being courageous and facing difficult situations.

Start Time: 26 minutes, 22 seconds

Where to Begin: Kuzco and Pacha are outside Pacha's home, and Kuzco says, "I don't make deals with peasants."

Where to End: Kuzco is backed to the edge of a cliff, facing a pack of jaguars. Pacha swings on a rope, saying, "Don't worry your highness; I gotcha. You're safe now."

Plot: When a wicked advisor turns Emperor Kuzco into a llama, Pacha, a kindhearted peasant, helps Kuzco get home. Kuzco initially insists he needs help from no one, but eventually sees his need for Pacha.

Review: The builders of the Tower of Babel were as self-centered and egotistical as Emperor Kuzco. Just as Kuzco thought the world revolved around him and that he needed no one, the tower builders desired to make a name only for themselves and left God out of their lives. Use this clip to help children relate Kuzco's need for Pacha with our need for God.

Supplies: Writing paper, pencils, and LEGO blocks or other small blocks

NOW PLAYING

Have children form pairs. Tell the children to come up with a new language for counting from one to ten. Provide pairs with paper and pencils, then allow children several minutes to create gibberish words for the numbers. Be sure kids write the numeral (1, 2, 3 and so on) next to the matching gibberish word. Have them write the new name for the number next to the appropriate number. After the children have finished, ask one person in each pair to hold onto the paper with the numbers and names but not to allow other children to see the paper. Form new pairs such that no two children who were together before are matched again and such that only one person in a pair has a sheet of paper. Give each pair a few blocks.

Say→ Now that we have names for our numbers, we're going to work in pairs to build towers. The person holding the paper will say, "Stack ___ blocks." Fill in the blank with one of the words from your paper. Your partner will have to try and figure out the matching number. Your partner may ask you which number, and you may shake your head "no" or nod your head "yes," but you can't give any other clues. When your partner figures out the correct number, he or she may stack that many blocks to form a tower. Let's see who can build the tallest tower.

Let children play for about three minutes, then see which pair has the tallest tower. If time permits, let the children with papers hand over the "code" to their partners, then remix the children and play again.

Ask→ • How difficult was it to know which number of blocks your partner wanted you to use?

• How do you think that's like trying to communicate with someone who speaks a different language from yours?

• Could you have worked faster if you both spoke the same language?

Say→ The Bible tells about a group of people who wanted to build a tower to the heavens. The group became very vain and self-centered—they thought of no one but themselves and left God out of their lives. The builders thought they didn't need God. So God confused their language. He made them speak different languages so that it was difficult for them to talk to one another. They couldn't communicate, so they couldn't build this man-made tower to the sky. The place they were building the tower was later called Babel.

Let's watch a clip from *The Emperor's New Groove*.

Show *The Emperor's New Groove* clip.

Ask→ • How is the emperor like the builders of the Tower of Babel?

• How does the emperor feel when he's facing all of the hungry jaguars?

• How do you think he feels when Pacha rescues him?

Say→ Kuzco thought he didn't need Pacha, just like the builders of the tower thought they didn't need God. Kuzco eventually learns the lesson that he needs others. We can learn from this movie clip and especially from this Bible story that we always need God.

ABRAHAM IS TESTED (1)

Scripture: Genesis 22:1-18

 Movie Title:
SHILOH (PG)

The Critics Say — Use this movie to discuss issues of sacrifice, selflessness, and integrity.

Start Time: 1 hour, 24 minutes, 38 seconds

Where to Begin: Jud drives off with Shiloh.

Where to End: Shiloh runs back to Marty. Marty's father says, "I think you've got yourself a dog."

Plot: Marty helps a runaway dog named Shiloh recover from his injuries. The dog's owner, Jud, discovers Shiloh's whereabouts, and agrees to let Marty "earn" Shiloh by doing odd jobs. Marty keeps his end of the bargain, but Jud doesn't.

Review: Focus kids' attention on Marty's feelings and his decision. Marty provided for Shiloh's needs and worked hard to earn Shiloh. Marty had the "right" to keep Shiloh, just as Abraham had the "right" to keep his son. But Abraham trusted God's plans, even if he didn't understand them.

Supplies: Blindfolds, paper plates, carrot sticks, pudding cups, and spoons

Allergy ALERT

Preshow: Keep the snacks out of sight.

NOW PLAYING

Say→ I'm going to give everyone a snack, but wait for my directions before eating.

Distribute carrot sticks on paper plates.

Say→ You have a choice to make before eating. You can either eat the carrots or give them up and accept the new snack that I'll give you. You can't ask any questions about the new snack. If you want to keep your carrots, pull your plate toward you. If you want to give them up for an unknown food, gently push the plate away.

After children have indicated their choices, give those who were brave enough to trust you for a new snack the pudding cups and spoons. Ask children to still wait before eating their snacks.

Ask→ • How did you make your choice about trusting me for a new snack?

• How did it feel to give up your snack for something unknown?

• What are other situations where you need to trust others?

• What kinds of things do we need to trust God to do for us?

Let children eat their snacks. Let kids who want to trade for a different snack do so.

Say→ We're going to watch a scene from *Shiloh*. Marty has helped a runaway dog recover from injuries and has even agreed to earn Shiloh by doing twenty hours of work for Shiloh's cruel owner, Jud. But Jud goes back on the agreement and demands to have Shiloh back.

   Show the clip from *Shiloh*.

Ask→ • How did Marty feel about giving up Shiloh?

   • What do you think Marty was fearful of?

Say→ It seemed wrong to return Shiloh to an abusive owner. Marty still trusted that it was the right thing to do. The Bible tells us about a time when God asked Abraham to trust him in an unusual way. God wanted Abraham to sacrifice his son, Isaac. Abraham must have felt that offering Isaac didn't make sense either, but he trusted that God's plans always work best. Both Abraham and Marty gave up their loved ones, and, in the end, both were rewarded by receiving them back again.

ABRAHAM IS TESTED (2)

Scripture: Genesis 22:1-18

 Movie Title:
SPIRIT (G)

You can also use this clip to teach about freedom.

Start Time: 1 hour, 11 minutes

Where to Begin: Spirit and the boy come to the rise overlooking the village.

Where to End: The boy whoops with happiness, and Spirit and Rain run off together.

Plot: Spirit still longs to be free, so the boy sacrifices Spirit and his own horse, Rain, in order to allow the two horses to run free.

Review: Use this scene to help children understand the great sacrifices God may ask us to make.

 Supplies: Markers and small flat stones

NOW PLAYING

Ask→ • What does it mean to sacrifice something?

   • Have you ever sacrificed anything? Explain.

Say→ We're going to watch a scene from *Spirit*. In this scene, we'll see an American Indian boy making a big sacrifice.

   Play the clip.

Ask→ • What sacrifice did the boy make?

   • Why do you think he made this sacrifice?

Say ➔ Now I'd like to share a story with you about another sacrifice.

Read Genesis 22:1-18 aloud, or tell the story in your own words.

Ask ➔ • What would you have thought if God asked you to give up someone you loved so much?

• What would you have done if you were in Abraham's shoes?

Have students form trios, and ask trios to discuss the following questions.

Ask ➔ • What sacrifices have others made for you?

• What sacrifices have you made for others?

• Why do you think people make sacrifices?

Have trios share some of their ideas with the entire group.

Say ➔ Wow—you have some great ideas about sacrifice! In the story of Abraham and Isaac, we saw that God didn't actually end up requiring Abraham to sacrifice his son. God only desired Abraham to be faithful and obey him, even when it didn't make sense to Abraham. In the same way, God wants us to commit to trust him and follow him, even when the things he asks us to do don't make sense or require great sacrifice.

To remind us of this and to help us make commitments to trust and obey God, we're going to create "commitment stones." I'd like each of you to take a flat stone that can remind you of the stone in the story of Abraham and Isaac. On your stone, I'd like you to write or draw something that will remind you of your commitment to trust and obey God.

Give students time to do this. Encourage them to put their stones in a place where they'll see them every day as a reminder of their commitments.

JACOB GETS ISAAC'S BLESSING (1)

Scripture: Genesis 27:1-40

Movie Title:
THE LION KING (G)

Use this clip to teach about showing honor to those in authority.

The Critics Say

Start Time: 4 minutes, 10 seconds

Where to Begin: A mouse enters the cave.

Where to End: Scar says, "Oh, I shall practice my curtsy."

Plot: With the birth of Simba, Scar has no hope of inheriting the throne from his brother, Mufasa. Scar has conveniently "forgotten" to go to the celebration of Simba's birth, and Mufasa is now coming to confront him.

Review: Scar is jealous about Simba's birth and all the rights and privileges that come with that birth. As the movie unfolds he constructs a detailed plot to overthrow Simba and take back what he feels is rightfully his. Just as in the story of Jacob and Esau, the birthright has brought about jealousy, deception, and deceit.

Supplies: Chalkboard eraser and masking tape

Preshow: Use masking tape to create three lines on the floor. Make one line in the center of your playing area, and create a line on either side of the center for the two teams to stand behind.

nOW PLAYING

Say➜ **In this game you'll try to take something that another person thinks belongs to him or her.**

Form two equal teams, and have each team number off so that each child has a number. There should be one child on each team with the same number as a child on the opposing team. Have the teams line up on the outer lines, facing one another. Place the eraser on the center dividing line. Call out a number, and have the two children with that number run and try to get the eraser and make it safely back to their team before the other person gets the eraser or tags them.

Play until everyone has had a chance to have his or her number called at least once. You can also call several numbers at the same time to have four or more children racing for the eraser. Then have children return to their seats.

Ask➜ • **How did you feel when someone took what you thought belonged to you?**

• **How did you feel when you were the one who took the eraser from someone else?**

Say➜ **In the movie *The Lion King*, Scar believes that Simba has stolen what is rightfully his. Let's watch and see what happens.**

Show *The Lion King* movie clip.

Ask➜ • **What kind of feelings did Scar have toward Simba?**

• **Why did Scar feel this way?**

• **How are Scar's feeling like the feelings you had when you were playing the game? How are they different?**

Say➜ **I'd like to tell you a Bible story about two brothers. One brother took something that didn't belong to him, and the other brother was very angry.**

Tell the story of Jacob and Esau from Genesis 27:1-40.

Ask➜ • **How did Esau feel when he found out that Jacob had stolen his birthright?**

• **How is that like what Scar felt toward Simba? How is it different?**

• **What can you do when you feel someone has taken something from you?**

• What should you do if you are the one who's taken something that doesn't belong to you?

JACOB GETS ISAAC'S BLESSING (2)

Scripture: Genesis 27:1-40

Movie Title:
ALADDIN (G)

The Critics Say

> You can also use this clip to teach children about respecting the property of others.

Start Time: 1 hour, 9 minutes

Where to Begin: Aladdin says, "I've gotta tell Jasmine the truth."

Where to End: Iago flies away with the lamp.

Plot: Jafar has sent Iago to steal the lamp from Aladdin, so that he can receive the wishes from the Genie. Iago tricks Aladdin into thinking Jasmine is calling him. When Aladdin leaves Iago sneaks in and gleefully steals the Genie's lamp.

Review: You can use this scene to help children understand that God wants us to do the right thing. Just as Iago pretended to be Jasmine in order to get the lamp from Aladdin, Jacob pretended to be Esau to get Isaac's blessing. When Jacob stole Esau's blessing from Isaac, he took what rightfully belonged to his brother. So Jacob's actions were selfish and deceitful. God wants us to do the right thing and not lie to get something that belongs to someone else.

Supplies: Red and green construction paper, glue sticks, scissors, black markers, and craft sticks

NOW PLAYING

Say→ We're going to watch a scene from *Aladdin*. Aladdin knows that he needs to do the right thing and be honest with Jasmine and tell her who he really is. But Jafar, the evil sorcerer, wants the lamp and has sent his parrot, Iago, to get it for him. Let's watch and see what happens.

Show the *Aladdin* clip.

Ask→ • How do you think Aladdin felt about having deceived Jasmine into thinking he was a prince?

• How do you think Iago felt about deceiving Aladdin into thinking he was Jasmine?

• Was either one doing the right thing? Why or why not?

Say→ To help us remember when to do the right thing, we're going to make Stop and Go signs.

Have each child cut one circle from the red paper and one from the green paper. To make sure the circles are the same size, lay the two sheets of construction paper together, and cut the circles from both sheets at the same time. Show children how to glue the two sheets together, placing the craft stick at the bottom as a handle. Then have kids write STOP on the red side and GO on the green side.

Say→ **God wants us to do what's right. In our Bible story, we have two brothers, Jacob and Esau. Esau was the firstborn son and, therefore, was entitled to his father's blessing. Jacob deceived his father into giving him the blessing by pretending to be Esau. This hurt everyone involved. The Bible tells us in 2 Thessalonians 3:13, "never tire of doing what is right." Use your Stop and Go signs as a reminder that we should stop doing the things that are wrong and always do the things that are right.**

Let children take turns naming situations where they could choose to do the right or wrong thing. Let others respond with their signs to show which actions they would choose.

JOSEPH IS SOLD BY HIS BROTHERS

Scripture: Genesis 37:1-36

Movie Title:
HARRIET THE SPY (PG)

You can use this clip to teach children that God has a plan for everything that happens in our lives.

The Critics Say

Start Time: 24 minutes, 30 seconds

Where to Begin: Harriet and Mr. Waldenstein are having a stare-down at the dinner table.

Where to End: Harriet, Miss Gully, and Mr. Waldenstein sit down at the movie.

Plot: Miss Gully has invited her friend Mr. Waldenstein over for dinner. Harriet isn't quite sure about this man. When Miss Gully burns the bratwurst, Mr. Waldenstein calls it a blessing in disguise because now they can all go out to dinner and a movie.

Review: Use this clip to show how God can take things that might seem wrong in our lives and make something good out of them. It's his blessings in disguise that make life exciting. Joseph could have given up when his brothers sold him into slavery. Instead he let God use him for greater things. And in later years, Joseph surprised his brothers with blessings.

Supplies: Paper plates, hole punches, ribbon, markers or crayons, and scissors

Preshow: Cut the paper plates in half, and snip out a triangle in the middle of the cut edge to fit over the nose of a child.

NOW PLAYING

Give each child half of a paper plate, and make markers or crayons available.

Say→ Think of someone who is special to you or someone who makes your life better. Then use your paper plate to make a mask so you can disguise yourself as that person. The triangle cutout will go over your nose, and you can cut out eyeholes and use markers or crayons to make your mask.

As children finish their masks, help them punch holes in the sides of the plate and use the ribbon to tie the masks around their heads.

Ask→ • How does this person help you or make your life better?

• Would you say this person is a blessing to you? Why or why not?

Say→ We're going to watch a scene from *Harriet the Spy*. Harriet and Miss Gully are having dinner with a friend when something goes wrong. Let's watch.

Show the clip from *Harriet the Spy*.

Ask→ • Have you ever had a "blessing in disguise," which is something that went wrong at first but ended up being good? If so, what happened?

• How did it make you feel?

Say→ When Joseph's brothers sold him into slavery, it was a terrible time. Joseph had no idea what God had in store for him. God turned this situation into a true blessing in disguise. Because of what happened to him, Joseph was able to help his family and his whole nation! God always knows what is best for us.

Ask→ • How do you feel when something doesn't go the way you'd like it to?

• Do you trust God to work things out? Why or why not?

• Should we trust God to work in our lives? Why or why not?

• What would help you trust God when things aren't going how you've planned?

BIRTH OF MOSES

Scripture: Exodus 2:1-8

Movie Title:
AMERICAN LEGENDS (G)

The Critics Say

John Henry and Moses both led others through the wilderness to a new land. In fact the music used in the clip refers to Canaan, which was the Promised Land for the Israelites.

Start Time: 2 minutes, 15 seconds

Where to Begin: The quilt reads, "John Henry."

Where to End: The railroad is completed.

Plot: John Henry's wife recalls the folk hero's birth, childhood, and rise to leadership as a railroad worker during the period of western expansion.

Review: The song in this clip speaks of John Henry being born "with a hammer in his hand." In other words, John was born to lead the westward expansion of the railroad. Though Moses wasn't born with a staff in his hand, he was set apart from birth for the unique role of leading God's people out of slavery. Throughout this lesson, remind kids that God has a specifically designed plan for each one of them.

Supplies: Index cards, pencils, and basket

NOW PLAYING

Arrange kids in groups of about five or six. Distribute index cards and pencils. Have each group write three baby-related questions such as "On what day of the week were you born?" or "What was your first favorite toy?" Then have each group write three questions that could be answered by a child of their own age, such as "What do you like to do in your spare time?" or "What's your favorite movie?" Place all the questions in a basket.

Let one child draw a card and read the question aloud. Have other children answer the question *as they think the reader would answer the question* about himself or herself. After several children have guessed, let the reader answer the question correctly. Then have another child draw a card and play again. Play as long as time permits.

Ask➜ • **Based on what you know about yourself as a baby and what you know about yourself now, what do you think you'll be doing in twenty years?**

• **How might God let you know what your future holds?**

Say➜ Some of the interests and experiences you're having today will shape who you become in the future. Even things that happened to you as a baby— things like where you were born or how many brothers and sisters you have—make you who you are. Let's watch a movie clip about the birth of a folk hero named John Henry.

Show the movie clip.

Ask➜ • **How did John's childhood help him to become a leader?**

• **What did people admire about John Henry?**

Say➜ Moses didn't appear to be a "born leader" like John Henry. However, God designed the events of Moses' childhood to prepare him for leadership. At a time when Pharaoh commanded Hebrew baby boys to be killed, Moses was spared. He was discovered by an Egyptian princess and grew up well educated. Later, he rejected his royal upbringing and worked as a shepherd. God used these events to shape Moses into a man who would lead people through deserts and to the land God promised them. You may not realize it, but God is shaping your life, too!

GOD CALLS MOSES

Scripture: Exodus 4:10-12

Movie Title:
THE PRINCESS DIARIES (G)

You could also use this lesson to help children understand that God can take a life and transform it.

Start Time: 10 minutes, 11 seconds

Where to Begin: The Queen welcomes Mia to tea and says, "Amelia, I'm so glad you could come."

Where to End: Mia storms off after telling her grandmother that she doesn't want to be a princess.

Plot: Mia has been asked to tea by her grandmother, whom she has never met. She surprises Mia by announcing that Mia is a princess.

Review: Use this lesson to help the children understand that when God asks us to do something that we may not think we are capable of doing, he will give us the strength, courage, and wisdom to accomplish it. When we say yes to God, we have him to guide us.

Supplies: Construction paper and markers

now PLAYING

Place the supplies where children can reach them. Explain that they'll each make an advertising poster to promote a "Say Yes to God" campaign.

Say→ **If you wanted others to know how they can say yes to God or why they should do this, you might make an advertisement!**

Allow kids time to create their posters and then show them to each other.

Say→ **We're going to watch a scene from *The Princess Diaries*. Mia is going to meet her grandmother for the first time.**

Show the clip.

Ask→ • **How would you react if someone told you that you were the only living heir to the throne of a country you had never been to?**

• **How do you feel when someone asks you to do something you don't think you can do?**

Say→ **God gives us many opportunities in life. Some of them we know we can do; some of them may be a bit harder. But God would never ask us to do anything that he didn't think we could do. He is always there to help us out.**

Many leaders from the Bible felt that they weren't the right people for the job God had given them. In fact, in Exodus 4, God called Moses to be a leader, and Moses argued that he couldn't do it! But with God's help, Moses and other leaders accomplished wonderful things. Likewise if we say yes to God and let him work in us, we can do great things too.

Ask➜ • What kinds of things would you like to do for God?

• How do you feel when you do something that you never thought you could?

• How do you think God feels when we say yes to him and trust him to help us?

GOD PROMISES DELIVERANCE

Scripture: Exodus 6:1-8

 Movie Title:
THE EMPEROR'S NEW GROOVE (G)

Use this clip to teach children about betrayal and true friendship.

Start Time: 39 minutes, 25 seconds

Where to Begin: Kuzco and Pacha begin walking over the bridge. Pacha says, "OK, once we cross this bridge it's only an hour to the palace."

Where to End: When Pacha says quietly, "You just saved my life."

Plot: The young Emperor Kuzco is immature and enjoys mistreating his subjects, including a peasant named Pacha. When Kuzco's evil advisor turns him into a llama out of revenge, he's befriended by the kindhearted Pacha.

Review: This clip illustrates that God is more trustworthy than humans who, in this clip, turn out to be sneaky and conniving.

Supplies: Blindfolds and obstacles in the classroom such as a chair, table, and desk

nOW PLAYING

Have children form pairs, then blindfold one child in each pair. Place obstacles in the room that the children will need to avoid while they make their way from one end of the room to the other.

Say➜ Direct your blindfolded partner by guiding him or her with only your voice around the obstacles I've placed in the room. You may start wherever you are, but you need to have your blindfolded partner walk completely around each obstacle. When you're finished with the last obstacle, switch places and do the activity again.

Let pairs complete the obstacle course. Watch out for any kids having trouble. When the children are finished, have them sit down.

Ask➜ • What was easier, being able to see and directing your blindfolded partner or not being able to see? Explain.

• How hard was it to trust your partner?

• How is that like or unlike trusting God to lead you?

Say➜ We're going to watch a scene from *The Emperor's New Groove.* Kuzco has befriended Pacha, or so it seems. Let's see which one is the better or more trusting partner.

Show the clip.

Ask➜ • How do you think Pacha felt when he was betrayed by Kuzco?

• Who was the better friend to the other? Why?

Say➜ The Bible is full of God's promises. Let's read one.

Read Exodus 6:1-8.

Say➜ God kept this promise and brought the Israelites to safety. We can still trust God today to keep his promises.

CROSSING THE RED SEA

Scripture: Exodus 13:17–14:31

 Movie Title:
THE LAND BEFORE TIME V: THE MYSTERIOUS ISLAND (G)

The Critics Say

You may also use this video to discuss helping others.

Start Time: 1 hour, 4 minutes

Where to Begin: Littlefoot says, "Our families—not that we'll ever see our families again."

Where to End: The adult dinosaurs thank Elsie for saving their children and all say goodbye.

Plot: While searching for food, young dinosaur friends Littlefoot, Cera, Spike, Ducky, and Petrie become stranded on an island. When all hope of finding their families seems gone, a swimming dinosaur gives them a ride across the water.

Review: God had shown his power to the Israelites over and over again. Yet when faced with one more difficult situation, the Israelites grumbled that they'd have rather died in bondage in Egypt than in freedom in the desert. God once again showed his mighty power by allowing Moses to part the Red Sea so they could cross to safety. In this clip, the dinosaurs are rescued in a mighty way as well. Use this clip to discuss that no matter how big our problems seem, God can always solve them.

Supplies: Blue gelatin, wax paper, plastic knives, and bear-shaped cookies.

Allergy **ALERT**

Preshow: Before class prepare the blue-colored gelatin, chilling until set. Just before class cut rectangles of gelatin, 2x4-inches, and place each one on a strip of wax paper.

NOW PLAYING

Say→ Let's watch a scene from *The Land Before Time V: The Mysterious Island*. The dinosaur friends are trapped on an island away from their families. Let's watch.

> Show *The Land Before Time* clip.

Ask→ • How do you think the dinosaurs felt about their difficult situation?

• What do you do when faced with a big problem or difficult situation?

Say→ There's a story in the Bible about a group of people who were faced with a very difficult situation. God helped Moses rescue the Israelites from being slaves in Egypt. But now, the Israelites seemed doomed to being recaptured. They were caught between a huge sea of water and the Egyptian army. Just as the swimming dinosaur rescued the young dinosaur friends, the Israelites are rescued in a mighty way. God helped Moses part the waters, and the Israelites walked right through on dry land.

Let's reenact this story from the Bible using a yummy snack.

> Give each child a gelatin rectangle. Let the children use the plastic knives to cut the gelatin in half and slide the two pieces away from each other. Then let children use their Israelite people (bear-shaped cookies) to "walk" through the sea on dry ground.

Ask→ • How do you think the Israelites felt about their difficult situation?

• How did God solve their problem?

• Who can you turn to when you have a difficult situation or problem?

Say→ Try to remember that no matter how big our problems are, God can always help us.

THE TEN COMMANDMENTS

Scripture: Exodus 20:1-17

> You can also use this clip to discuss rules.

Movie Title:
BABE (G)

Start Time: 23 minutes

Where to Begin: The scene begins with an overhead shot of one of the dogs, Rex, in the barn speaking to all of the farm animals.

Where to End: When Rex's speech is finished.

Plot: Babe and the duck plot to get rid of the alarm clock, but everything goes wrong, and they get in trouble. Rex, the leader of the animals, "lays down the law" in this scene.

Review: Children are used to having rules stated and enforced, but they may think people in authority create rules that are senseless.

God's rules keep us safe and help us know how to live. Use this scene to spark discussion about rules children must follow and the reasons behind those rules.

 Supplies: Index cards and pens or pencils

now PLAYING

Ask→ • What rules do you have to follow in your life?

• What rules seem silly to follow?

• Do you think rules are important? Why or why not?

Say→ In this scene from *Babe*, Rex, the leader of the farm animals, shares new rules he's created with the other animals to keep them out of trouble.

Play the clip.

Ask→ • What do you think about Rex's rules?

• Why do you think Rex created these rules?

Say→ Just as Rex shared new rules with the animals, Moses shared God's new rules, the Ten Commandments, with the Israelites. Following the Ten Commandments lets people live in peace with each other and with God.

Rex's rules turned out to be not very good ones, but God's rules help us know how to treat God and others.

Let's think about rules we're asked to follow in our lives.

Have students form pairs. Give each pair an index card and a pen or pencil.

Say→ With your partner, write down one rule that you or others are asked to follow at home, school, work, or in sports.

Give pairs about a minute to think and write, then collect the cards. Shuffle the cards, and redistribute them to the pairs.

Say→ Read your new card, and discuss what might happen if someone broke this rule. You've got two minutes to talk.

After discussion, allow a few of the pairs to share their rule and what might happen if this rule were broken.

Ask→ • Why do you think it's important to follow the rules?

• How can understanding the consequences of breaking rules make it easier to follow them?

Say→ It might seem like rules just limit us and keep us from doing what we want to do. But rules are important! God gives us rules to keep us safe and help us live together in harmony.

CALEB TRUSTS GOD

Scripture: Numbers 13:1-32

 Movie Title:
HONEY, I SHRUNK THE KIDS (PG)

> You can use this movie clip to teach children about fear, trusting God, and friendship.

The Critics Say

Start Time: 28 minutes

Where to Begin: The kids tear open the garbage bag and discover they're in the backyard.

Where to End: Nick says, "I don't think we're in the food chain anymore, Dorothy."

Plot: A father accidentally shrinks his own kids and those of his neighbor when his homemade science experiment goes awry. The kids, shrunk to the size of insects, suddenly must learn how to survive in a gigantic world where the objects they used to take for granted are now menacing dangers.

Review: You can use this clip to show kids how scary it must have been for most of the Israelite spies when they realized how big the Canaanites were in the land they were to invade. Watching this clip will give kids the perspective of being very small in a very big world, which is how many of the Israelite spies felt after their venture into the Promised Land. Caleb, unlike most of his peers, was undaunted by the size and apparent strength of the Canaanites. He trusted God and knew that God would stand by his promise of giving them the land he had led them to.

 Supplies: 3-foot length of rope or clothesline for every two kids

NOW PLAYING

Say➜ When Caleb and the other Israelite spies snuck into Canaan to scope out the land God had promised them, they must have been surprised at what they saw. Surprised and scared. The people there were way bigger than they had anticipated. Even the *fruit* was huge! They felt like little bugs.

Let's watch a clip from the movie *Honey, I Shrunk the Kids* to see how those spies must have felt.

Play the movie clip.

Ask➜ • How do you think the kids felt when they realized how small they were?

• How is that like how you think the spies felt in Canaan?

• When do you feel like something in your life is impossible?

Say➜ Most of the spies came back with the report that taking the land God had promised them was impossible. The people there were just too big and too powerful. But not all of the spies felt that way. Caleb knew that God could help them with the job of taking over the Promised Land even though it seemed impossible. Let's try an experiment about doing something that seems impossible.

Have kids form pairs, and give each pair a length of rope.

Say→ OK, here's the impossible task. Hold one end of the rope in each hand, and tie a knot without letting go of either end. Take turns with your partner as you try to figure out a solution together.

Give kids several minutes to try.

Say→ It may seem impossible to tie the knot without letting go of the ends, but it can be easily done. Here's how.

Explain that the trick is to fold your arms first and then have your partner hand you the two ends of the rope. When you unfold your arms, a knot will form in the center of the rope. Give kids another few minutes to practice the trick.

Say→ This trick seemed impossible at first, but it actually could be done. Taking over the Promised Land seemed impossible to most of the spies, but Caleb trusted God to help them. He knew that with God, nothing is impossible!

BALAAM'S DONKEY

Scripture: Numbers 22:21-31

Movie Title:
DOCTOR DOOLITTLE (1967) (G)

You also could use the clip to teach about listening to God.

The Critics Say

Start Time: 29 minutes

Where to Begin: Dr. Doolittle stands up from his desk and begins speaking with his parrot.

Where to End: Dr. Doolittle talks to the pig.

Plot: Dr. Doolittle, a medical doctor, discovers that he can hear and understand the conversation of animals. The talking animals help him realize that he'd much rather be a veterinarian who helps animals, rather than a people doctor .

Review: You can use this clip to demonstrate how God can use anyone and anything to draw us closer to him. It took talking animals to help Dr. Doolittle realize what was important in his life. In the same way, it took a talking donkey to get Balaam's attention and turn his attention back to God. Help kids see that God can use anyone—even them—for his divine purposes.

Supplies: Paper cups, water, plant, stickers, markers, and glitter glue

Preshow: Crumple one paper cup without putting any holes in it. The cup should still be useful but should look disheveled and worn. Set the other cups and craft supplies out of sight.

now PLAYING

Say→ We're going to watch a clip from *Doctor Doolittle*. Dr. Doolittle gets some advice from a surprising source. Let's watch.

Show the *Doctor Doolittle* clip.

Ask→ • How did the talking animals help Dr. Doolittle?

• How do you think Dr. Doolittle's life changed after learning to speak to the animals?

Say→ Dr. Doolittle got some help and advice from an unusual source—talking animals! In the Bible a man named Balaam got some help from a talking donkey. God used the donkey to get Balaam's attention and turn him back to God.

God can use anyone and anything to get our attention and turn us back to him. You may not think God can use you, but you're wrong. If God can use a talking donkey, he can surely use you! Even if you're young, or shy, or scared, God can use you. Let me show you what I mean.

Gather kids around the plant you brought.

Ask→ • What does this plant need to stay alive?

• What would happen if it didn't receive those things?

Say→ Let's pretend that this plant is really, really thirsty. It hasn't had a drink in weeks. It's about to die. And the only container I have to put water in is this crumpled old cup.

Ask→ • Do you think this plant would care whether I used a crumpled cup? Why or why not?

• What would happen if I were only willing to use a perfect cup?

Say→ The plant would die without water. The plant wouldn't care what the cup looked like; it wouldn't care whether the cup was perfect or not. It's sort of the same with people. People need to hear about Jesus. Unless they do, they'll have to spend eternity without God.

God can use you to tell people about him. It doesn't matter if you're not perfect. God can use you, just like I can use this crumpled cup.

Fill the crumpled cup with water, and give the plant a drink.

Say→ Let's make something to remind us that God can use anyone—even you!

Give each child a cup, and set out the craft supplies for kids to share. Encourage kids to decorate their cups in ways that will remind them of the story of Balaam and the talking donkey.

RAHAB SAVES THE SPIES

Scripture: Joshua 2:1-22

You can use this clip to teach kids about telling the truth.

The Critics Say

Movie Title:
E.T.: THE EXTRA-TERRESTRIAL (PG)

Start Time: 33 minutes, 40 seconds

Where to Begin: The mom says, "Kids, I'm home," and Elliott, his brother, and unwilling sister quickly hide E.T. before their mother enters the bedroom.

Where to End: After the mother leaves without noticing E.T.

Plot: Elliott has discovered and made friends with E.T. and decides to introduce him to his brother. Just after the introduction, their little sister enters the room, which causes everyone (including E.T.) to start screaming. Just then they hear their mother coming, and Elliott and his brother quickly clamp a hand over their sister's mouth and hide E.T. The mother enters and leaves the room without discovering E.T.

Review: You can use this scene to introduce kids to the idea of hiding someone, just as Elliott hid E.T. and Rahab hid the spies. This clip will help kids sense the danger and apprehension Rahab and the spies must have felt when the soldiers were approaching for their search.

Supplies: Map of your classroom, treats, and transparent tape.

Allergy ALERT

Preshow: Hide a container of treats somewhere in your classroom. Then draw a map of the room with a meandering line that leads to an X that marks the spot where the treats are hidden. Tear the map into as many pieces as there are children in class. (If you have a large class, make sure to draw the map on paper large enough to give each student a readable piece of the map.)

NOW PLAYING

Give each child a piece of the map you prepared before class. Tell kids to keep their pieces private.

Say→ **I gave each of you a piece of a map that leads to some treats I've hidden in the room. In a little while, I'll let you hunt for the treats. But first, let's watch a scene from the movie *E.T.* Elliott has discovered E.T. and is trying to hide him from his mother. Let's see what happens.**

Show the movie clip.

Ask→ • How did Elliott keep his mother from finding E.T.?

• How do you think Elliott felt when his mother opened the closet door?

• How do you think E.T. felt?

Say→ Elliott and E.T. were probably nervous and scared that E.T. would be discovered. Elliott tried his best to hide E.T., but he didn't know whether his help would be enough. That must be a lot like how Rahab and the spies felt when she hid them on her roof. They could probably hear the soldiers getting closer and closer, and they were probably scared they would be discovered.

But they were safe because of Rahab's help. They could never have hidden from the soldiers themselves. They needed help, just like E.T. needed Elliott's help. Let's see what it's like to need help! You'll need your map pieces.

Explain that each child has a piece of a map of the classroom. On the map, the location of the hidden treats is shown. Kids will have to figure out how to help each other find the treats.

Set out tape for kids to use as they work to piece the map together. When the map is whole, let kids find the treats. As kids enjoy the treats, remind them that no one could have found the treats with just a little piece of the map. They needed each other's help, just as the spies needed Rahab's help and E.T. needed Elliott's help.

DAVID AND GOLIATH

Scripture: 1 Samuel 17:1-50

Movie Title:
A BUG'S LIFE (G)

Use this clip to teach that children can stand together for what's right.

The Critics Say

Start Time: 1 hour, 17 minutes, 40 seconds

Where to Begin: Hopper picks up Dot, and she screams.

Where to End: When the ants chase the grasshoppers away.

Plot: Even though the ants do all the work, the grasshoppers have come to claim what they feel the ants owe them. In this scene Flick stands up to Hopper, and the entire ant colony stands behind him, banishing the grasshoppers forever.

Review: David must have felt tiny in comparison to Goliath, yet he trusted God would use him and would bring victory. Use this scene to help kids realize that no matter how small or helpless they may feel, God always has a job for them to do.

now playing

Say→ In this scene from *A Bug's Life,* Flick, the ant hero, stands up to Hopper, the leader of the grasshoppers. The much smaller Flick defeats Hopper and the other grasshoppers with the help of the ant colony.

Play the clip.

Ask→ • What do you think you would have done if you were Flick in this situation? Explain.

• Have you ever been asked to do something that you didn't feel you were big enough to do? What happened?

Say→ Even though Flick was so much smaller than Hopper, he defeated Hopper with the power of all of the ants. This reminds me of the story from the Bible about David and Goliath. David was a young man, but God gave him the power to defeat Goliath—a giant that adults were too afraid to fight. Because David trusted God and his power, he beat Goliath even though he was so much smaller. Let's play a game of Shrink Tag to help us remember that God will give us the power we need to do any job.

Choose one person to be It. Explain that this game is similar to Tag, except that when It tags someone, that person has to "shrink" or crouch down. The tagged person can still move around; he or she just has to stay crouched down. It's job is to "shrink" as many people as possible. The other players can touch a tagged person and "enlarge" him or her. Play until It is tired, and then play another round with another It.

Ask→ • How did it feel to be "shrunk" by It in this game?

• How did it feel to be "enlarged" again by one of your teammates?

• How did it feel to "enlarge" someone else?

Say→ Just as we gave each other the power to be big enough to do what needed to be done in this game, God gives us the power to do the job he wants us to do. I'd like for you to remember this during this next week, especially when you're faced with a task that seems too hard or too "big" for you.

DAVID AND JONATHAN (1)

Scripture: 1 Samuel 20:1-42

Movie Title:
MONSTERS, INC. (G)

Scene 1 Start Time: 57 minutes, 25 seconds

Where to Begin: Mike says, "Uh, Sir, that's not her door," and Sulley and Mike are banished to the Himalayas.

Where to End: When Mike says, "You're on your own," and Sulley turns to sled off to town.

Scene 2 Start Time: 1 hour, 5 minutes

Where to Begin: Randall, who can become invisible, is fighting with Sulley.

Where to End: When Mike realizes what has been happening and says, "Hey! Look at that! It's Randall! Ooh."

Plot: Sulley has been trying to help Boo, the little girl who has wandered into Monstropolis, get back to her room. As a result, he and his friend Mike have been banished into the Himalayas. This has an impact on their friendship.

Review: You can use this scene to help children understand what it means to be a real friend. At first Mike was hurt that Sulley risked their lives in order to save the little girl. He questioned Sulley's loyalty, wondering if their friendship meant anything. Mike later realized that their friendship was important, and he supported Sulley in his efforts to save Boo. David and Jonathan's friendship was based on trust and understanding of each other. David's life was in danger, and Jonathan risked his own life to protect his friend.

 Supplies: Paper and crayons or markers

noW PLAYInG

Have children fold their papers in half. On the front flap, have them draw a picture of something they like to do. On the inside flap, have them draw something their friends like to do.

Ask→ • Do the things you like to do and the things your friends like to do ever conflict or get in the way of your friendship? If so, what do you do?

• What things can get in the way of friendships?

Say→ We're going to watch two short scenes from *Monsters, Inc.* In the first scene we see Sulley and Mike banished to the Himalayas. The next scene will show us the interaction between Mike and Sulley once they get back to Monstropolis. Let's watch.

Show the *Monsters, Inc.* clips.

Ask→ • Why do you think Mike was so upset with Sulley?

• How would you feel if your friends weren't spending time with you in order to do something else they thought was important?

• How do you think Sulley felt when Mike told him he was "on his own this time"?

Say→ In the Bible account of David and Jonathan, Jonathan's father was angry with David and wanted to kill him. Jonathan risked his life to protect his friend. Because of Jonathan, David lived. David and Jonathan vowed to always be friends.

Ask→ • In what ways is Sulley and Mike's friendship like David and Jonathan's?

- **How can we be the kind of friend who's always there for another?**
- **Who is someone you can befriend?**

Say→ God wants us to be friends who can be trusted. Mike and Sulley were that kind of friend. David and Jonathan were that kind of friend. With God's help, and with Jesus at the center of our friendship, we can be that kind of friend, too.

DAVID AND JONATHAN (2)

Scripture: 1 Samuel 20:1-42

Movie Title:
ICE AGE (PG)

Use this clip to teach the children about faith and trust.

The Critics Say

Start Time: 1 hour, 18 seconds

Where to Begin: The animals are cleaning the baby as they walk through the snow.

Where to End: Diego says to Manny and Sid, "Because I'm your only chance."

Plot: Manny, Sid, and Diego are supposed to be taking the baby to his family. Diego knows of an ambush by the other saber-toothed tigers up ahead, and he warns his new friends, Manny and Sid, about it.

Review: Jonathan and David were unlikely friends, as Jonathan had the right to the throne, but he recognized that God had given the throne to David. No one would have been surprised if they were enemies, yet they loved each other and looked out for each other. In this movie, an unlikely friendship has formed between a variety of animals, and they must learn to rely on each other. Use this scene to teach children about friendship and how friends look out for each other.

The Critics Say

Emphasize trusting people children know. Be careful not to give kids a false sense of security about trusting strangers.

Supplies: Yellow card stock, tape, craft sticks, and red markers

Preshow: Cut the card stock into $8\frac{1}{2}$-inch squares.

NOW PLAYING

Have the red markers and tape available for the children. Give each child a yellow square and a craft stick. Then have them make a border around their square with the red marker. Have them turn their square so that it is a diamond shape and write the word "Warning!" in the center. Tape the craft stick onto the back so it can be held up like a sign.

Say→ We're going to watch a scene from *Ice Age.* Manny, Sid, and Diego are trying to find the baby's family. Diego knows of some danger ahead. When we get to the part where Diego warns them about the danger, hold up your signs. Let's watch.

Play the clip from *Ice Age*.

Ask→ • Why do you think Diego warned Sid and Manny about the danger?

• Why do you think Sid and Manny questioned Diego about why they should trust him?

• Would you trust him?

Say→ Diego spends time with Sid, Manny, and the baby, and as Diego spends time with them, he begins to care for them as friends. He cares more for them than his standing with the other saber-toothed tigers. Because of this friendship, Sid and Manny could trust Diego to warn them about the danger that was ahead.

The Bible tells us about two friends named David and Jonathan. When Jonathan found out that his father wanted to harm David, he knew he had to warn David even if that meant going against his father. David knew he could trust Jonathan because of their friendship. Friends look out for one another.

Ask→ • Do you have a friend who you know you can trust?

• Can your friends trust you?

• Would you be willing to warn a friend who you knew was going to do something to harm him or herself?

Say→ We need to be willing to help our friends even if it's not the popular thing to do. We need to be a friend who can be trusted.

DAVID AND MEPHIBOSHETH

Scripture: 2 Samuel 9:1-12

Movie Title:
LIKE MIKE (PG)

You can also use this clip to illustrate the importance of being loved or having a family.

Start Time: 1 hour, 29 minutes, 30 seconds

Where to Begin: Calvin is shooting baskets at the orphanage. A boy approaches him and says, "What was the best part about being in the NBA?"

Where to End: Tracy says, "That's right, we're going home!"

Plot: Calvin is a fourteen-year-old who's had his ultimate wish fulfilled to play in the NBA. Although he becomes an instant NBA celebrity, he remains alone and orphaned until this final scene.

Review: David showed kindness to Mephibosheth, even though it was not required of him. In this clip, NBA star Tracy Reynolds chooses to show great kindness by adopting two children—even though it's not required of him either.

Supplies: Newsprint, tape, and crayons

Preshow: Tape the newsprint around the walls so children can reach it.

now PLAYING

Ask→ • Did you know that when you're not in this room, it's cleaned and picked up by someone?

• Have you ever thanked the people who do this?

• What are some ways to thank them?

Say→ Let's write thank-you notes on these papers and leave them for the people who clean this room for us.

Allow time for the class to write thank-you notes on the newsprint. Leave these for the cleaning staff. If time permits, choose one or more of the other ideas children thought of, and show thanks in these ways as well.

Ask→ • What is kindness?

• How does it feel when you show kindness to someone?

• How does it feel when others are kind to you?

Say→ We're going to watch a scene from *Like Mike*. A young orphan named Calvin has just experienced the thrill of a lifetime—he got to play in the NBA. But he's still an orphan. Watch and see how someone shows him kindness.

Show the *Like Mike* clip.

Ask→ • Who showed kindness to Calvin?

• How do you think Calvin felt about this kindness?

Say→ There is a story in the Bible about a time David, the king of Israel, showed kindness to a crippled relative of his long-dead friend Jonathan.

Tell the story found in 2 Samuel 9:1-12.

Ask→ • Why do you think David wanted to show kindness to Mephibosheth?

• What do you think Mephibosheth felt when he learned what David had planned for him?

• Who are people you can show kindness to?

• What specific actions can you do this week to show them kindness?

Say→ Our thank-you notes are an act of kindness, and the people who clean this room show us kindness by their actions too. Let's do our best to show kindness to everyone we can!

SOLOMON'S WISDOM

Scripture: 1 Kings 4:29-34

Movie Title:
THE WIZARD OF OZ (G)

> You could use this movie clip to teach children about talents, individuality, and gifts from God.

> The Critics Say

Start Time: 36 minutes, 20 seconds

Where to Begin: Scarecrow says, "Oh, I'm a failure because I haven't got a brain."

Where to End: Dorothy and Scarecrow set out together on the Yellow Brick Road.

Plot: As Dorothy heads down the Yellow Brick Road on her way to Oz, she comes across a scarecrow who wishes he had a brain. Dorothy invites the scarecrow to accompany her to Oz, where she says the wizard there will surely help the scarecrow with his problem.

Review: Solomon knew he wasn't smart enough to effectively rule the people of Israel without God's help. So instead of asking for riches and power, he asked God for wisdom instead. In a way, he was like the scarecrow in the movie, who valued knowledge and learning enough to travel to Oz and ask the wizard for wisdom.

Supplies: Paper and pencils, calculator, and chalkboard and chalk or large sheet of newsprint and a marker

Preshow: If you don't have a chalkboard, tape a large sheet of newsprint to a wall where everyone will be able to see it.

nOW PLAYING

Say→ I'm feeling very wise today. How about you? Do you feel wise? Let's see how wise you are! I'm going to show you an amazing math trick I can do, and I want to see if you're wise enough to figure out how I did it. I'll need a volunteer.

Have a volunteer join you at the chalkboard or newsprint. Have the volunteer write any five-digit number on the board. Under the number, write your own five-digit number, apparently at random. But actually, you'll choose your digits so that each one, added to the number above it, equals nine. For example, if the volunteer writes 45623, you would write 54376.

Then tell your volunteer to write another five-digit number under your number. Then you write a fourth number, using the same nine-principle method as before. Have your volunteer write a fifth number, then draw a line under it.

Say→ Watch how wise I am! I'll add all these numbers in no time! I'll even write the answer from right to left!

Subtract two from the fifth number that was written, and put a 2 in front of the resulting number. That's your total, and it looks as though you added it in your head! (For example, if the fifth number written was 48765, the number you write as the total is 248763.) Then let a volunteer quickly add the numbers on a calculator to verify that you wrote the correct number.

Say➔ **Amazing, isn't it? How did I add those numbers so quickly? Find a partner, and see if you can figure it out.**

Have kids form pairs or trios, and let them try to figure out how you added the numbers so quickly. Have paper and pencils handy for kids to use. Be prepared to repeat the math puzzle again if kids want you to. After a few minutes, call time.

Say➔ **It looked like I was so wise that I could add like a calculator. But it was just a trick.**

Explain how the trick was done.

Say➔ **See? I wasn't so wise after all!**

Ask➔ • **What exactly does it mean to be wise?**

• **Who's the wisest person you know? Why did you choose that person?**

Say➔ **Let's watch a movie clip about someone who wanted very badly to be wise. See if you remember this character from *The Wizard of Oz*.**

Show the movie clip.

Say➔ **In the movie the scarecrow was convinced he wasn't smart and he needed a brain. So he decided to go ask the Wizard of Oz for help. In a similar way, Solomon knew he needed help to rule the people of Israel. He knew he wasn't smart enough to do a good job on his own. So he asked God for wisdom. He could have asked for anything at all—money, power, riches—but he knew he needed wisdom. And he knew the only one who could give it to him was God.**

The next time you feel like the scarecrow, like you're in need of a brain, do what Solomon did. Ask God for some wisdom!

ELIJAH AND THE PROPHETS OF BAAL

Scripture: 1 Kings 18:16-39

 Movie Title:
THE VELVETEEN RABBIT (NOT RATED)

Use this clip to help the children understand the difference between man's "magic" (optical illusions) and God's miracles.

Start Time: 20 minutes

Where to Begin: The stuffed rabbit sheds a real tear.

Where to End: The rabbit is leaping and jumping for joy at having been turned into a real rabbit.

Plot: A stuffed rabbit toy, loved and cherished by a young boy, has been told he would become real if he were truly loved by the boy. When the boy becomes ill with scarlet fever, all of his belongings must be destroyed. The rabbit is crushed to know that he can never be with the boy again.

Review: Use this clip to teach that only God can perform miracles. In *The Velveteen Rabbit*, the Nursery Fairy changes the stuffed animal into a real rabbit. We all know this story is pretend and could not really happen. However, God does perform a miraculous, seemingly impossible feat through Elijah when he causes fire to come down from heaven and burn up the wet altar when Elijah calls on God.

Supplies: Balls or beanbags that can be juggled

Preshow: Locate someone within your church or community who can juggle, and schedule this person to come to your class on the day you intend to use this clip.

now playing

Give several children three balls, and ask them to juggle the balls. After the children struggle to juggle for a minute or more, allow other children in the class to attempt juggling. Then introduce your guest, and have him or her juggle.

Ask→ • How hard was it for you to juggle the balls?

• Was it impossible for our guest to juggle balls?

Say→ Sometimes we can see someone doing something that we think is impossible! It may not really be impossible, just hard for us to do without practice. If someone taught you how to juggle and you practiced a lot, you, too, would be able to juggle.

We're going to watch a scene from *The Velveteen Rabbit* about an event that could never really happen, no matter how much someone practiced! Let's watch to see what I'm talking about.

Show the clip from *The Velveteen Rabbit*.

Ask→ • Even with practice, could you ever learn to turn a stuffed rabbit into a real rabbit?

Say→ No, you're right—we could never turn a toy into something real. That's just a pretend story. In the Bible there's a story about something God did that seems like it would be impossible to do. Elijah wanted to prove to the people that God was the one true God. Elijah built an altar and soaked it in water, lots and lots of water. And he told the people that he was going to call on God to cause a fire on the altar. This seemed like an impossible task—the altar was completely soaked, and the wood shouldn't have burned. But God is all-powerful and mighty and can do many wonderful, miraculous things, things that seem impossible to us. Elijah called on God, and he sent fire from the heavens that burned up the wet altar! God can do amazing things!

Let's practice our juggling again. This task may seem impossible to us, but it's really not if we practice and have a good teacher! Let's let our guest teach us to juggle.

Have your guest teach the children to juggle, and have them practice. Remind the children often that this skill sometimes takes quite a while to perfect.

NEHEMIAH

Scripture: Nehemiah 2:17-20

Movie Title:
🎥 HOMEWARD BOUND II: LOST IN SAN FRANCISCO (G)

This clip is great for teaching about loyalty to God, serving others, and being courageous.

Start Time: 47 minutes, 10 seconds

Where to Begin: A mother is screaming for her son, Tucker, who's caught in a burning building.

Where to End: Tucker thanks Sassy for saving his cat and thanks Shadow for saving his life.

Plot: Shadow goes into a burning building to save a human while the other dogs ridicule his loyalty. Shadow ignores them and saves the human, and Sassy follows him, knowing that it's the right thing to do.

Review: Just as Shadow and Sassy are loyal to humans, we can be loyal to God, even in the face of danger. Nehemiah knew that loyalty too. Jerusalem had crumbled, and even though the people who were loyal to the king were ridiculing him, Nehemiah and the other Jews began building a wall to show their loyalty to God.

Supplies: Bible, construction paper, markers, and masking tape

Preshow: Before the meeting, tear sheets of construction paper in half widthwise to make "bricks." Make sure you have about three or four bricks per child. You'll also want to clear off a wall in your room.

NOW PLAYING

Say→ Today we're going to watch a movie clip about a dog who didn't pay attention to what others were saying around him.

Show the *Homeward Bound II* clip.

Ask→ • Why do you think Shadow and Sassy went into the fire for someone they didn't really know?

• Why do you think Shadow and Sassy were so loyal to humans?

• Do you think God wants us to be loyal? or courageous? Why or why not?

Say➜ Shadow didn't pay attention to the other dogs who thought he was crazy for risking his life for a human. Shadow was courageous and loyal. Let's hear about someone else who was also courageous and loyal. His name is Nehemiah. When Jerusalem had crumbled, Nehemiah knew that God would want the Jews to rebuild it. So he ignored what others were saying and started to rebuild the wall.

Read aloud Nehemiah 2:17-20. Then hand out bricks and markers. Tell the kids to write one action on each brick that is an act of loyalty to God. As kids write on the bricks, "stack" them by taping them to a wall.

Say➜ Shadow and Sassy showed their loyalty to a human by saving him in the fire, and Nehemiah showed his loyalty to God by building a wall. We can show loyalty, too, by doing all of these things and more. When we help someone, or when we pray, or when we follow God's rules, we are loyal. And even when our lives are at stake or when people make fun of us, we can still be loyal because we know that God's love is stronger than anything.

PSALM 23 (1)

Scripture: Psalm 23

Movie Title:
🎥 **BEAUTY AND THE BEAST (G)**

> Young children may find the wolf attack scene frightening, so use discretion in showing this clip.
>
> *The Critics Say*

Start Time: 46 minutes

Where to Begin: Belle says, "I can't stay here another minute" and leaves the castle.

Where to End: The Beast looks at Belle and collapses after fighting off the wolves.

Plot: Belle has had enough of the Beast's temper and being held prisoner, so she attempts to escape. Out in the snow, alone, she is attacked by a pack of wolves. While standing in the middle of the pack, fighting them off with a stick, the Beast comes to her aid and fights the wolves off for her. The wolves eventually flee from the area completely and Belle is safe.

Review: You can use this scene to help children understand that God will always protect them. Even though Belle had run away, the Beast still sought after her and protected her. In the same way, God seeks after us and protects us.

Supplies: Cotton balls, black construction paper, toothpicks, hole punch, and glue

NOW PLAYING

Give each child one cotton ball and two toothpicks. Have each child punch three holes from black construction paper and save the tiny dots. Show children how to make a sheep from these items by gluing two of the black dots onto the cotton ball as eyes and one as a nose. Then have kids break their toothpicks in half and dip one end of each toothpick half into a small amount of glue and stick them into the cotton ball as the sheep's legs.

Say→ We're going to watch a scene from *Beauty and the Beast.* Belle is being attacked by wolves and is scared and needs help. Let's watch.

Show the *Beauty and the Beast* clip.

Ask→ • What do you think Belle was thinking when she saw she was surrounded by wolves?

• How do you think Belle felt when she saw the Beast helping her?

Say→ God wants us to know that just like the Beast was there to help Belle, he is always there to help us, no matter what the situation is.

Belle was in a dangerous situation. The Beast, caring for Belle, came to her rescue, fought off the wolves, and saved her life. God does that for us. Psalm 23 talks about the Lord being our Shepherd. A shepherd is responsible for taking care of his sheep and for protecting them. One of the things a shepherd needs to watch out for are wolves attacking his sheep! Just like a shepherd watches out for his flock, the Lord watches out for us.

Ask→ • How is God's protection like the Beast protecting Belle from the wolves?

• How is it different?

• What are some things God protects you from?

Say→ The sheep we made today can be reminders to you that God will always protect you.

PSALM 23 (2)

Scripture: Psalm 23

 Movie Title:
QUEST FOR CAMELOT (G)

Use this clip to discuss the abilities of people with disabilities.

Start Time: 33 minutes, 30 seconds

Where to Begin: Kayley and Garrett leave the forest and wander into the land of dragons.

Where to End: Garrett pulls Kayley into a large broken egg to hide from dragons.

Plot: Kayley, daughter of a knight, takes it upon herself to find King Arthur's sword, Excalibur, after it has been stolen by an evil knight. Kayley is aided by an unlikely hero, a blind squire named Garrett.

Review: Though Kayley doesn't realize it, Garrett is protecting her. Though we don't always stop to think about it ourselves, God guides and protects us "through the valley of the shadow of death." Use this clip to remind children that God is always with us.

now PLAYING

Say→ Let's watch a scene from *Quest for Camelot*.

Show the clip.

Ask→ • Can you describe the forest?

• Who helped protect Kayley from the dangers of the forest?

• What are dangers in our world?

• How does God protect you?

Say→ Let's learn a rap to remind us of Psalm 23.

Say the rap, line by line, clapping to keep the rhythm. Have the children echo the words back to you until they can say it along with you. Let children add creative noises and sounds to the rhythm of the beat, if they choose.

The Lord is my shepherd,
And I am the sheep.
He watches over me,
My life, he does keep.
To grass—soft and green,
Beside the waters still.
Down the righteous path,
My cup, he will fill.
My cup overflows,
With goodness and love.
And all my blessings come,
From God, the Lord above.

Encourage kids to remember this rap and Psalm 23 when they're facing fears or uncertain times.

THE FIERY FURNACE (1)

Scripture: Daniel 3:1-30

 Movie Title:
THE ARISTOCATS (G)

Use this clip to teach students that God can protect them.

Start Time: 1 hour, 10 minutes, 10 seconds

Where to Begin: Roquefort calls, "Mr. O'Malley!" as he chases after the cat.

Where to End: Roquefort yells, "Hey! Wait for me!" as he and the cats run to save Duchess and the kittens.

Plot: After O'Malley thinks he has delivered Duchess and the kittens safely back home, Roquefort discovers Edgar's evil plot to send

Duchess and the kittens to Africa. O'Malley sends Roquefort to find Scat Cat. As a mouse, Roquefort is terrified of Scat Cat, but he goes anyway.

Review: It must have been scary for Shadrach, Meshach, and Abednego to stand up to the king, yet they knew it was what God wanted them to do, and they obeyed. Use this scene to help kids realize that even though God may ask them to do some big or scary things, if they put their trust in him, God will keep them safe.

Supplies: White card stock; orange, red, yellow, and black crayons; and toothpicks

now PLAYING

Ask➜ • Have you ever had to do something really scary? What were you thinking and feeling?

Say➜ Right now, I'd like to show you a scene from *The Aristocats.* In this scene Roquefort, the mouse detective, has just discovered an evil plot to send Duchess and the kittens to Africa. He runs after O'Malley to get him to help rescue the cats. O'Malley sends Roquefort to find Scat Cat and the other cats to help. Roquefort is terrified of Scat Cat, but he does as O'Malley asks.

Play the clip.

Ask➜ • What do you think you would have done if you were Roquefort in this situation? Explain.

Say➜ Roquefort was really scared of Scat Cat, but he went to find him because he knew that if he didn't, Duchess and the kittens might not be rescued. In the Bible there's a story of three men who faced something even scarier—they were put into a fiery furnace because they believed in God. Even though they could have died in the fire, these men stood strong and did what they were told to do. God kept them safe in the fire, and they weren't even burned! Just as these men could trust God to keep them safe, we know that we can trust God to help us through even the most difficult or scary situations.

Let's create a fire picture to remind us that God kept the men safe even in a fiery furnace.

Give each child a sheet of white card stock. Set out the red, yellow, orange, and black crayons. Show children how to use the "fiery colors" to cover the card stock with color. Make sure they press down hard as they color to make the colors very strong and vibrant. After they've finished coloring the fire colors, have them cover the entire sheet with black crayon. Again, tell them to press hard as they color, and make sure they cover the whole sheet well so that no colors show through the black.

When they're finished, give each child a toothpick, and tell children to scratch a picture of the fire and the men in the fire.

THE FIERY FURNACE (2)

Scripture: Daniel 3:1-30

Movie Title:

OUR FRIEND MARTIN (NOT RATED)

You can also use this clip to teach about racism.

Start Time: 21 minutes

Where to Begin: The boys travel through time and when they arrive, Randy asks, "Where are we now?"

Where to End: Martin says, "It's called a boycott."

Plot: Randy and Miles are assigned a school project on Martin Luther King Jr. They are traveling through time, experiencing King's life as he lived it. They have just landed in Montgomery, Alabama where Rosa Parks has refused to give up her seat on a city bus. The African American community has decided to boycott the bus system.

Review: A boycott means that you will not be participating in a particular activity. In this movie clip, the African American community has taken a stand against something they think is unfair and incorrect. In the same way, Shadrach, Meshach, and Abednego boycotted King Nebuchadnezzar's statue and refused to bow down to anyone or anything but God.

Supplies: White paper, markers or crayons, paint stirring sticks (many stores will give you these for free), and tape

Preshow: Make a sample "boycott" sign by writing the word *boycott* on a piece of paper and then taping it to a stick. Also, think of several scenarios the children might find themselves in. Some of them should be things they should boycott (such as, cheating, swearing, bullying, and skipping church to play). The others should be things that they should not boycott (such as obeying their parents, being kind, attending church, and doing community service).

NOW PLAYING

Say➔ We're going to watch a scene from *Our Friend Martin*. Randy and Martin have landed in Montgomery, Alabama where a bus boycott has just begun. Let's watch and see what happens.

Show the *Our Friend Martin* clip.

Ask➔ • What is a boycott?

• When does a boycott work?

- Do you think that the African Americans were right in boycotting the bus system?

Say→ There were three young men who boycotted something in the Bible. Let's read about them and see what they boycotted.

Tell the story of Shadrach, Meshach, and Abednego from Daniel 3:1-30.

Ask→ • What did these three young men boycott?

• How is what they did, like what the African Americans did in Montgomery?

• How is it different?

• What are things we might want to boycott?

Hand out the supplies to make the boycott signs, and have each child make one.

Say→ We are going to play a game. I am going to give you a situation, and if you think you should boycott it hold your sign up high in the sky. If you think it is something that is OK for you to do, keep your sign down.

Go through each scenario, randomly choosing between things kids might or might not boycott. After each scenario, ask a few children to tell you why they did, or didn't boycott that situation. Let children share possible scenarios too, and let the others respond to them.

DANIEL IN THE LIONS' DEN

Scripture: Daniel 6:1-28

Movie Title:
DISNEY'S THE KID (PG)

You can also use this scene to teach the children that it's not necessary to bow to peer pressure.

Start Time: 1 hour, 21 minutes, 33 seconds

Where to Begin: The kids are running out to recess.

Where to End: Rusty walks through the gate and calls, "Here I come!"

Plot: Rusty is confronted by the school bullies who he knows he'll have to fight. But because Russ is there with him, he knows he can handle the situation.

Review: Daniel had to have courage to stand up to the men who tried to bully him into bowing to their desires instead of the desires of God. In this clip, Rusty gains courage to do what's right because his grown-up self, Russ, is with him. Use this scene to teach the children that we can have courage to stand up for what is right because God is with us.

NOW PLAYING

Say➜ We're going to watch a scene from *Disney's The Kid.* Rusty has a decision to make. He can either stick up for what's right and confront the bullies, or he can back down and let the bullies have their way. Let's watch and see what he decides to do.

> **The Critics Say**
>
> You'll want to make sure to stop the video before the fight scene. The point of this lesson is that Rusty has courage because he knows what he is doing is right and that Russ is with him.

Show the clip.

Ask➜ • How do you think Rusty felt?

• What would have you done if you were Rusty?

• Do you think Rusty did the right thing? Why or why not?

Say➜ Rusty knew that what the boys had planned was wrong. But he also knew that if he opposed them, he could get hurt. Yet he decided to do what was right and help the dog.

The Bible tells us Daniel knew that what the king wanted him to do was wrong. Daniel knew we are only to pray to and worship God. He also knew that if he didn't do what the king said, he would be thrown into a den of lions. Yet he did what was right. Knowing that God would be with him gave Daniel the courage to do what was right.

Have children form small groups, and ask each group to act out a situation where they might be asked to do something wrong and have to choose to stand up for what's right. Allow a few minutes for each group to prepare, then have the groups take turns performing their skits. Have all the children return to their seats.

Ask➜ • Have you ever had to choose to do something that was right, even though it might not have been the popular thing to do?

• Were you afraid to do the right thing?

• How did you feel after it was all over?

Say➜ We should never be afraid to do what is right because we have the promise that God is always with us.

JONAH AND THE BIG FISH

Scripture: Jonah 1–4

 Movie Title:
HOMEWARD BOUND (G)

> **The Critics Say**
>
> Use this clip to teach about friendship or role models.

Start Time: 36 minutes

Where to Begin: Shadow and Chance are looking out over the river at twilight, and Shadow says, "I shouldn't have made her come."

Where to End: Chance says, "I just hoped that one day I could be like him."

Plot: Two dogs, Shadow and Chance, and a cat, Sassy, are trying to make their way back home to their family. The three attempted to cross a river, and while Shadow and Chance made it across, Sassy didn't and was swept over a waterfall. The dogs think she's lost forever. In this scene, Shadow reflects on his responsibilities as a dog, both to Chance and Sassy and to his family.

Review: Jonah learned that obedience was his responsibility, and God expects the same from us. Use this scene to help kids realize that when they become followers of God, they're given certain responsibilities. The biggest responsibility of all is simply following God and acting in obedience.

Supplies: One sheet of newsprint for each child, tape, and markers

Preshow: Tape the sheets of newsprint around the room.

NOW PLAYING

Ask→
- What does it mean to have responsibility or to be responsible?
- What things are you responsible for in your life?

Say→ I'd like to show you a scene from *Homeward Bound.* In this scene, the two dogs, Shadow and Chance, discuss the responsibilities that come with being a dog.

Play the clip.

Ask→
- According to Shadow, why do dogs do these things?

Say→ Shadow does his best to fulfill his responsibilities. The story of Jonah shows us a man who, at first, didn't do what God wanted him to do. He didn't fulfill his responsibilities as a follower of God.

Tell the story of Jonah in your own words.

Say→ Let's think about the responsibilities we have in our lives. I'd like you to think about two areas of responsibility—your responsibilities to God and your responsibilities to people.

Choose a newsprint sheet on the wall. Find a marker and along one side of the paper write "My Responsibilities to People." On the other side, write "My Responsibilities to God." Under each heading, jot down as many responsibilities as you can think of. For example, under the first heading, you might write something like "To do my homework every night." Under the second heading, you might write something like "To worship God." Take a few moments to write down everything you can think of.

When students have finished, go around the room, and have them share what they wrote. Then have them discuss how they can fulfill their responsibilities to God and to other authority figures.

JOHN POINTS TO JESUS

Scripture: Matthew 3:1-11

Movie Title:
TOY STORY (G)

You can also use this clip to illustrate teamwork.

The Critics Say

Start Time: 8 minutes, 47 seconds

Where to Begin: Woody says to the army toys, "Sergeant, establish a recon post downstairs."

Where to End: The kids run out of the bedroom, and the closet door creaks open.

Plot: A new toy threatens to take over the most favored status of Cowboy Woody. In this clip all the toys work together to spy on Andy, their owner, and see what new toys will be joining them in Andy's room.

Review: What does anticipation feel like? It can be the nervous tension just before a test, the sleepless night before a campout, or the long wait before Christ returns. Many children haven't considered the anticipation of Christ's return, so this clip provides the emotional connection to help them think about what's in store for them as Christians.

Supplies: Paper and markers or crayons

now PLAYING

Ask→ • Have you ever felt nervous because you couldn't wait for vacation?

Say→ On the piece of paper, draw a line in the center dividing the paper into two equal parts. On one side draw a picture of what your face looks like the night before you're going to leave on a vacation. On the other side draw a picture of what you're face looks like a few minutes before you take a test at school.

Allow time for the picture drawing.

Say→ Show your picture to your neighbor, and see if that person can tell which face is the night before a vacation and which is a few minutes before a test. Allow a few minutes for children to interact.

Anticipation can be good, and it can be bad! In the following movie clip, watch how the toys anticipate and prepare for the discovery of the new toy in the house.

Show the *Toy Story* clip.

Say→ I know, you want to see their reaction don't you? It's hard to wait, and sometimes we get so nervous with anticipation that we can't even sleep. Many people in Jesus' day were waiting for a Messiah, the chosen one who would come to solve all their problems. Many people thought the Messiah would be John, and so they came to follow him. Listen to what John says.

Read Matthew 3:1-11 aloud, or retell the account in your own words.

Ask➜ • **What did the people feel when they heard that John was not the one they were looking for?**

• **What if I told you that at any second, Jesus could come back to meet us? How would you feel?**

• **Which side of your paper would your face look like? Why?**

Say➜ Anticipation makes us nervous because we don't know what to expect. The toys in the movie were afraid they would be boxed up and put in storage because of the new toy's arrival. John probably had the same reaction to Jesus' coming that we have today...he might have been nervous or wondered what would happen next! But we can rest assured knowing that Jesus is coming again, and that will be a very exciting time!

THE BEATITUDES (1)

Scripture: Matthew 5:1-12

Movie Title:
HOMEWARD BOUND (G)

> You can also use this clip to teach about the prodigal son.

The Critics Say

Start Time: 1 hour, 14 minutes

Where to Begin: Three kids and their stepdad are playing basketball outside. Jamie, the youngest child, turns around and says, "Did you hear that?"

Where to End: Shadow and Peter are reunited.

Plot: The family thinks that their pets, Shadow, Chance, and Sassy, have been lost forever. They're moving on in their lives, but they're still sad. In this scene, the three animals return to the family against all odds.

Review: Use this scene to help kids realize God will bless them, even during times of suffering and sadness.

NOW PLAYING

Say➜ To begin, I'd like to show you a scene from *Homeward Bound*. The family thinks their pets have been lost forever, and they're sad. Let's see what happens.

Play the clip.

Ask➜ • **Have you ever found something you thought was lost? Explain.**

Say➜ Before this movie scene, this family was quite sad because they thought they'd lost their beloved pets. But in the midst of their sorrow, they experienced tremendous blessings and joy when their pets were returned to them. In the same way, God offers blessings to people who experience all kinds of emotions. Let's read about it.

Read Matthew 5:1-12 aloud, and then reread verse 4.

Say→ In this passage, Jesus is standing on top of a mountain, speaking to his followers. Here he teaches them about how God blesses them. In verse 4, he says "Blessed are those who mourn, for they will be comforted." Those who mourn are people who may have experienced great loss in their lives, and they may feel like there's no hope. This verse tells us that God will comfort these people. Wow!

Have students form pairs.

Say→ Think of a situation in which someone who mourns might receive God's blessing. In the movie clip, mourning people were comforted. How else might mourning people be comforted? Take a few minutes to think of a situation.

When each pair has thought of and discussed a situation, have pairs join with another pair, and have each pair tell the other pair what they've discussed. Then allow a few pairs to share with the entire group. Remind kids that God is always there to comfort us in times of sadness.

THE BEATITUDES (2)

Scripture: Matthew 5:8

You can also use this clip to teach children about changed lives.

The Critics Say

Movie Title:

SPY KIDS (PG)

Start Time: 1 hour, 16 minutes

Where to Begin: A large group of robot kids is walking toward the Cortez family, and the family members lift their fists to prepare for a fight.

Where to End: Fegan Floop ruffles Juni's hair and says, "Thank you."

Plot: Robot children have been programmed to take over the world for their devious master. Siblings Carmen and Juni Cortez join forces with their spy parents to stop the robots. As they prepare to fight off the robots, Fegan Floop discovers he can alter the programming of the robots so their actions reflect pure motives.

Review: The robots are programmed so their actions reflect the heart and mind of their master. When Floop discovers he can change the programming so the robots follow a different master, the actions of the robot children are changed to the point that they rebel against their former master. Use this clip to teach children that when our hearts are pure, our actions reflect the desires of God.

Supplies: Bible, clear glass of water, red food coloring, and a tablespoon of bleach

now PLAYING

Show kids the clear glass of water, then have one of the children squeeze two or three drops of red food coloring into the water to demonstrate that the water is impure or no longer clean.

Ask➜ • **What would happen if I spilled this glass of water on a white shirt?**

• **Would the stain come out?**

• **Why or why not?**

• **What are things in our lives that can create an impure heart and mind?**

Have another child pour the bleach into the glass.

Ask➜ • **What happened when we added bleach to the impure water? What are things that can make our hearts and minds clean and pure?**

Say➜ In this movie clip, a group of robotic kids are about to destroy the Cortez family. Then something happens to change the robots' target. Let's see what happens.

Show the *Spy Kids* clip.

Ask➜ • **What did Fegan Floop discover could change the robotic kids?**

• **What happened when their minds were set to follow a new master?**

• **How does having pure minds and hearts change people?**

Read aloud Matthew 5:8.

Say➜ God desires for us to have pure hearts and minds so nothing stands in the way of our ability to love God. Let's ask God to help us keep our hearts and minds pure.

Close with prayer.

JESUS HEALS MANY

Scripture: Matthew 8:14-17

 Movie Title:
SLEEPING BEAUTY (G)

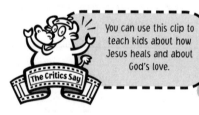

You can use this clip to teach kids about how Jesus heals and about God's love.

Start Time: 1 hour, 11 minutes

Where to Begin: The dragon has just died, and the prince walks into the castle courtyard.

Where to End: After Sleeping Beauty is kissed and has awakened.

Plot: A beautiful princess named Aurora has been cursed by an evil empress. The curse causes the princess to sleep as if in death. A charming prince awakens her with a kiss.

Review: You can use this scene to help kids visualize how Jesus healed so many people during his ministry, even people who were dead.

Everyone thinks Aurora, the beautiful princess, is sleeping the sleep of death, never to awaken again. But all it takes to cast off the spell and lift the curse is a kiss from the charming prince who loves her. Jesus loves *us* and has the power to heal us, both physically and spiritually.

Supplies: Paper clips, steel knitting needle, and large bar magnet

now PLAYING

Gather kids around a table on which you've placed the paper clips.

Say→ I have a little experiment to try. Watch this! I'm going to raise these paper clips with my knitting needle.

Try several times to lift the paper clips with the knitting needle. Obviously, it won't work.

Say→ Hmm. I must be missing something. Oh well, I'll try again later. Right now, let's watch a scene from the movie *Sleeping Beauty*. It's the part near the end where the princess is sleeping because of the evil curse that was put on her. No one can wake her up—she's just lying there like these paper clips.

Show the clip from *Sleeping Beauty*.

Ask→ • Why was everyone so sad about the princess?

• What finally caused the princess to wake up?

Say→ The princess was sleeping as if she were dead. No one could wake her up until the charming prince came along and kissed her. His kiss was the power that was needed to remove the curse so she could wake up.

The Bible tells us that during his ministry, Jesus healed lots and lots of people with his power. He even healed people everyone thought were hopeless, just like everyone in the movie thought waking the princess was hopeless. Jesus used his power to raise people from their sickbeds, and he still uses his power to heal people today. Hey, that gives me an idea!

Show kids the magnet.

Say→ Maybe all I need is some extra power to help me raise these paper clips.

Magnetize the knitting needle by holding the needle near the top and stroking the needle with the magnet. Be sure to move the magnet in one direction only and from about the middle of the needle to its tip. Do this ten to twenty times. Then pick up a paper clip with the needle.

Say→ See? All I needed was some outside power. The magnet transferred some of its power to the needle, and the needle was able to raise the paper clips. Jesus is the outside power we need whenever we have problems, whether it's because we're sick or because we have other problems. We can always count on Jesus to use his power to help us.

PARABLE OF THE SOWER

Scripture: Matthew 13:1-23

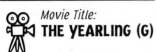

Movie Title:
THE YEARLING (G)

You can use this movie clip to teach kids about trusting God for provision.

Start Time: 1 hour, 43 minutes

Where to Begin: The bedridden father has to break the news to his son, Jody, that Jody's beloved pet deer has eaten the family's corn crop that they depend on for food.

Where to End: After Jody inspects the destroyed garden.

Plot: The Forrester family is trying hard to make a go of their small family farm during the post–Civil War era. Money is tight, and food is precious. Their son, Jody, has adopted a deer, a yearling, which has caused havoc in the family's garden.

Review: Food is a valuable and necessary commodity to the Forrester family. Their garden could mean the difference between life and death for the family. The yearling gets into the garden and ruins the corn so the plants will no longer grow and provide nourishment. In the same way, God's Word is like seeds planted in people's lives to provide life and nourishment. If the seeds can grow, so will faith.

Supplies: Potting soil, small rocks, several thorny stems, clear plastic cups, flower or vegetable seeds, healthy plant, water, and spoons

Preshow: Prepare three cups. In one cup, place good potting soil. In another, place the small rocks covered by a small amount of soil. In the third, place the thorny stems.

nOW PLAYING

Show kids the healthy plant.

Ask➜ • **Has anyone ever had a family garden? Or do you have plants at home?**

• **What helps a plant grow?**

Say➜ **Plants need help to grow, especially when they're starting out as seeds. They need water, sunlight, and good soil. Lots of things can go wrong when a plant is trying to grow.**

Let's look at a scene from the movie *The Yearling*. It's about a family that's trying to take care of its garden so they'll have food for the winter. But the son's pet deer is causing a lot of problems. Let's watch.

Show the movie clip from *The Yearling*.

Ask➜ • **Why was the family so upset in this scene?**

• **What did the deer do to the corn in the garden?**

Say→ The deer destroyed the corn crop—it was ruined and the plants would no longer grow. In the Bible Jesus compared the Word of God to little seeds that are trying to grow. He said that some seeds fall on the path and get eaten by the birds.

Sprinkle a few seeds on the table, then sweep them away with your hand.

Other seeds fall on soil that has rocks underneath it.

Show kids the cup with the rocks.

Other seeds fall among the thorns, and they get choked and can't grow.

Hold up the cup with the thorny stems.

But some seeds fall on good soil and produce wonderful crops.

Ask→ • What does it take for the Word of God to grow in a person's heart?

Say→ Just like the family in the movie prepared the soil for their seeds, tended their garden so the plants would grow, and shooed away the deer to protect the plants, we can tend the gardens of out hearts so God's Word can grow. We can pray and read our Bibles and listen to other Christians. That way God's Word can grow and grow in us! Let's plant some seeds to remind us that God's Word can grow in our hearts.

Give kids each a cup of good potting soil, and let them gently plant a seed in it. Help kids water their seeds, and encourage them to care for their plants at home to remind them that God's Word can grow in them.

JESUS WALKS ON WATER (1)

Scripture: Matthew 14:22-36

Movie Title:
THE PEBBLE AND THE PENGUIN (G)

Use this clip to talk about faith in God.

Start Time: 1 hour, 4 minutes

Where to Begin: Hubie sees his friend Rocko, after assuming he had been eaten by a whale, and Rocko calls, "Hey Romeo!"

Where to End: Marina hugs Hubie, and they fall down.

Plot: Hubie, the penguin, is lost at sea. Rocko, a rock-hopper penguin befriends Hubie and helps him find his way home. Rocko's one desire is to be able to fly. When Hubie is accosted by his rival, Drake, Rocko helps save the day by flying to Hubie's rescue.

Review: Most penguins cannot fly. It's an impossible feat for such birds. Walking on water is considered an impossible task for ordinary humans. But Jesus was no ordinary man! Use this clip to talk about Jesus' extraordinary capabilities because Jesus is God's Son.

Supplies: Chenille wires, craft sticks, scissors, low-temperature hot glue gun, water, and shallow pan

Preshow: Before class, cut or break craft sticks into 1-inch long pieces. Pour water into a shallow, low-sided pan, and set aside.

now playing

Ask→ • Have you ever tried to walk on water?

• Can you leap into the air and fly away?

• Can you change yourself into an animal?

Say→ You know, those are kind of silly questions, aren't they? Of course we can't do those things. Those things are impossible for us to do. Let's watch a clip about a penguin who thought it was impossible for him to fly. All of his life, he had wanted to fly. But, he just couldn't. Let's watch to see what happens.

Show *The Pebble and the Penguin* clip.

Say→ As you know, this story is just pretend. But, wouldn't it be fun to fly? That would be amazing! You know, the Bible tells us of many amazing things Jesus did. In one account, Jesus sent his disciples ahead of him in a boat. Later, Jesus went to meet them in the boat. Because the boat was already a great distance from shore, Jesus began walking on top of the water to get to the boat. How about that? He didn't even sink! Isn't Jesus amazing? When the disciples saw Jesus, they were so surprised! First they were frightened, then they couldn't believe their eyes. Peter even asked Jesus to let him come to him. So Jesus helped Peter walk on the water, too.

Let's make a puppet to help us remember that Jesus can do amazing things because he's God's Son.

Have the children use chenille wires to make small puppets. Make a loop at the top and twist the end around itself, forming a head. Bend the other end out slightly for a leg. Cut a piece and attach one end by twisting, forming the other leg. Wrap a longer piece around the middle, forming arms. Bend up hands and feet. Then have an adult use the hot glue gun to attach a piece of craft stick to each foot—sort of like a ski. Let the puppets stand to dry for several minutes. Then let the puppets "walk" on the water.

JESUS WALKS On WATER (2)

Scripture: Matthew 14:22-36

Movie Title:
HOMEWARD BOUND (G)

Start Time: 31 minutes

Where to Begin: A shot of a waterfall and rapids in the river.

Use this clip to discuss obedience.

The Critics Say

Where to End: Sassy is swept away, and Chance says, "Hang on Sassy!"

Plot: The three pets, Shadow, Chance, and Sassy, are trying to make their way home when they encounter a large river they must cross. The two dogs swim across and try to convince the cat, Sassy, to do the same. She refuses and finds her own way to cross on some rocks further downstream. Unfortunately, she slips and is swept away in the river.

Review: Use this scene to help kids understand that they can always have faith in Jesus, even in seemingly impossible situations.

Supplies: Small wading pool with water and a few inflatable water toys, rocks, and other things that will either sink or float

now PLAYING

Say→ I'd like to show you a scene from *Homeward Bound.* In this scene, the three pets need to cross a river. Let's see what happens.

Play the clip.

Ask→ • Why do you think Sassy should have trusted Shadow?

• Have you ever needed to trust someone in a scary or tough situation? What happened?

Say→ Just as Sassy needed to trust Shadow in order to cross the river safely, Peter needed to trust Jesus in order to walk across the water. As long as he was trusting Jesus and keeping his eyes on him, he could miraculously walk on top of the water just like Jesus. But as soon as he stopped trusting and got scared, he sunk into the water.

Point out the items, and ask students which ones they think will sink or float. Then encourage students to take turns experimenting with the items to see if they sink or float.

Say→ As you can see, some of these items sink in water. These items are just like we might be without trust in God. We could sink deep into despair and hopelessness. But if we trust God, he will help us float through problems, just like Peter could walk on water when he was trusting Jesus.

THE TRANSFIGURATION

Scripture: Matthew 17:1-8

Movie Title:
BABE (G)

Use this clip to teach students that God uses his power and love to transform people and situations.

Start Time: 1 hour, 22 minutes

Where to Begin: The scene opens with the clock starting to begin the sheep dog trial, and Mr. Hoggett says, "Away to me, Pig."

Where to End: The crowd goes wild with cheering.

Plot: Due to the unfortunate problems with Mr. Hoggett's prize-winning border collie, he doesn't have a dog to enter in the sheep dog trials. Through a series of events, he decides to enter his pig, Babe, instead. Everyone thinks Hoggett is crazy—until this final scene of the movie.

Review: This clip illustrates the change of attitude in the spectators as they see Babe in action. Use this scene to help kids understand that God's power and love can transform anything—even people's ideas and opinions.

Supplies: Several different items people might use to see, including magnifying glasses, binoculars, small telescope, kaleidoscope, reading glasses, 3-D glasses, and a clear glass of water

 Preshow: Set all of the items on a table.

now PLAYING

Say→ In this scene from *Babe*, we see Babe herding sheep by communicating with them. The crowd laughs at Mr. Hoggett, Babe's owner, for entering a pig in a contest that is reserved for dogs. Let's see what happens when the crowd sees Babe in action.

Play the clip.

Ask→ • What would you think if you saw a pig herding sheep?

• Have you ever been surprised by something someone did that you didn't expect?

Say→ Babe's incredible actions in this story changed, or transformed, people's ideas about pigs. In the Bible, God transforms Jesus in the eyes of the disciples; they finally see him as the true Son of God.

Explain to students that they're going to explore different ways of viewing things. Point out the items you've set out, and encourage students to experiment with the items, looking around at each other and the items in your classroom.

Ask→ • Which of these items were the easiest to see clearly through? Which were the most difficult?

• What item could you use to help you see God more clearly?

Say→ When God revealed Jesus' true identity to his disciples, he transformed their views and helped them to see clearly, just as Babe and Mr. Hoggett helped people to see the abilities of a pig more clearly.

THE TRIUMPHAL ENTRY

Scripture: Matthew 21:1-11

Movie Title:
MIRACLE On 34TH STREET (1947) (nOT RATED)

The Critics Say

You can use this movie clip to teach kids about praise and worship, about honoring God, and about joy.

Start Time: 6 minutes

Where to Begin: The parade begins.

Where to End: Santa has passed by, and the marching band is playing.

Plot: A little girl is jaded about Christmas and shows no enthusiasm for the celebration. Her mother, though, is coordinating the gigantic annual Christmas parade. All of New York, it seems, has turned out for the joyous parade and the arrival of its special guest, Santa.

Review: Use this movie clip to introduce the topic of celebration and joy to your class. In the movie, crowds of people turned out to watch the annual Christmas parade. The highlight of the parade, as always, was the special appearance of Santa Claus. The connection to Jesus' Triumphal Entry will be evident to kids—a parade, crowds of people, and a special appearance by a special guest!

Supplies: Variety of craft and household items which kids can use to make celebration instruments. Such items might include empty oatmeal boxes and coffee cans with lids (to make drums); cardboard tubes, dried beans, rubber bands and wax paper (to make rain sticks); and combs and wax paper (to make kazoos). You'll also need markers, stickers, tape, and curling ribbon streamers for kids to use to decorate their instruments.

Preshow: Cut the wax paper into squares large enough to rubber band around the ends of the cardboard tubes. (That size should also work for the kazoos.) Cut the curling ribbon into 12-inch lengths, and curl it yourself if you have mostly younger kids in class.

nOW PLAYInG

Ask→ • Has anyone here ever been to a parade? What was it like?

• Why do people have parades?

Say→ People have parades to celebrate important events or important people. There have been parades to celebrate the end of wars, to celebrate a president being elected, and even to celebrate a sports team winning a big title. Let's watch a scene from the movie *Miracle on 34th Street* to watch another kind of parade.

Show the movie clip.

Ask→ • What kind of parade was being held in the movie?

• Who was the guest of honor in that parade?

Say→ That movie clip reminds me of another parade, one in the Bible. The parade I'm thinking of is often called the Triumphal Entry, because it's when Jesus arrived in Jerusalem. Crowds of people gathered along the road and cheered for Jesus. They even laid down their coats and palm branches on the road for his donkey to walk on. It was quite a celebration! Let's make something to help *us* celebrate Jesus!

Set out the supplies, and explain that kids will be making instruments to play during their own parade. Let kids experiment with the supplies to make and decorate instruments.

If necessary, suggest instruments for kids to make. But if possible, let kids discover ways to make their own unique instruments.

After kids make and decorate their instruments, lead them in a parade around the church to celebrate Jesus, just as the people along the road to Jerusalem celebrated him. Encourage kids to take their crafts home to remind them that Jesus gives us a reason to celebrate!

PARABLE OF THE WEDDING BANQUET

Scripture: Matthew 22:1-14

You can use this clip to introduce the topics of acceptance, tolerance, and cliques.

Movie Title:
DUMBO (G)

Start Time: 9 minutes, 40 seconds

Where to Begin: The elephants gather around Mrs. Jumbo to see her new baby that the stork has delivered.

Where to End: Mrs. Jumbo closes the window on the laughing elephants.

Plot: Mrs. Jumbo, a circus elephant, has a special delivery—a brand new baby. All the elephants in the circus gather around her to see the new arrival. When Mrs. Jumbo unties the bundle, everyone sees that the new baby elephant has unusually large ears. All of the elephants, except his mother, make fun of little Dumbo. He's an outcast because he looks different.

Review: This scene where Dumbo is rejected because of his appearance should hit home for kids. It's a rare child who hasn't experienced the hurt of being made fun of because of some outward characteristic. Everyone can identify with Dumbo's rejection. Contrast that rejection, though, with the acceptance that Jesus shows for us. In the parable of the wedding banquet, Jesus tells the story of a king who ended up inviting even the most unlikely guests to his wedding banquet.

Supplies: Construction paper, fine-tipped markers, stickers, glitter glue, pens, and any craft items that kids can use to decorate invitations

now playing

Have kids form pairs to discuss the following questions. After each question, invite partners to share their answers with the rest of the class.

Ask➔ • **Have you ever felt rejected? Maybe someone made fun of you because of how you looked or what you were wearing. Or maybe your friend got invited to a party and you didn't. If that's ever happened to you, tell your partner about it.**

• **What feelings did you have when that happened to you?**

Say➔ **It's no fun to be rejected! Rejection can make us feel sad, embarrassed, or ashamed. Let's watch a scene from the movie *Dumbo* where the main character experiences rejection.**

Play the movie clip.

Ask➔ • **What happened to Dumbo in this scene?**

• **Why was Dumbo rejected?**

• **Do you think God ever rejects us because of how we look? Explain.**

Say➔ **God loves us and cares what we're like on the inside, not how we look! God wants everyone to be a part of his kingdom. In the parable of the wedding banquet, Jesus tells the story of a king who invited guests to a wedding celebration. When the guests didn't show up, the king invited all sorts of people—people you wouldn't think belonged at the king's house!**

That parable reminds us that God wants everyone to come to his kingdom. He would never reject anyone the way the elephants rejected Dumbo. God doesn't care how we look. He loves us and wants us to believe in Jesus so we can all come into his kingdom. Everyone's invited!

Let's make invitations to share with our friends. Think of someone who doesn't know Jesus. Then invite that person to get to know him!

Explain that kids can make invitations to church, invitations to talk about Jesus, or invitations to read certain parts of the Bible to learn about Jesus. Let kids decide how they want to invite others to get to know Jesus.

Set out the supplies you brought, and let kids design their invitations. After everyone's finished, let kids display them to the rest of the class. Encourage kids to follow through and give their invitations to the people they thought of. The next time you meet, ask kids how their invitations were received.

THE GREATEST COMMANDMENT

Scripture: Matthew 22:34-38

You can also use this clip to teach children about respect and caring for one another.

The Critics Say

Movie Title:
REMEMBER THE TITANS (PG)

Start Time: 31 minutes, 43 seconds

Where to Begin: The Titans are on an early morning run. They stop at the field where the Battle of Gettysburg was fought.

Where to End: Coach Boone finishes his speech to the young players.

Plot: The story takes place in West Virginia where a high school has just been integrated. A black head-football coach leads a team of both white and black players who initially do not like each other because of race.

Review: Use this clip to teach kids about the greatest commandment. Jesus taught that we are to love the Lord God with all our heart and to love our neighbor as ourselves. In this clip the coach tells his players that they may hate each other, but they will respect one another. God expects more from us to the point that in Matthew 5:44 we're to love our enemies.

 Supplies: Three or more types of fruit

NOW PLAYING

Have the children form threesomes. Give each threesome a piece of fruit, but tell the kids not to let the other groups know what kind of fruit that they have. Each group should brainstorm three facts they can give about the fruit. For example, for an orange they could say it has a peel that we don't eat, it can be made into a breakfast drink, and its color is orange.

Once all the groups have determined their three fruit facts, have them share those with the entire group and see if the group can guess the fruit.

Say→ We're going to watch a clip from *Remember the Titans*. In this scene the coach has led his football players on an early morning run. His goal is to help his players, both white and black, to learn to respect each other even though the color of their skin makes them seem different.

Show the *Remember the Titans* clip.

Ask→ • Why do you think people sometimes don't like each other simply because they have a different skin color?

• How are the differences in fruit like the differences in people?

Say→ In the Bible Jesus was asked what was the greatest commandment. This is how he replied in Matthew 22:37-40, " 'Love the Lord your God with all your heart and with all your soul and with all your mind.' This is the first and greatest commandment. And the second is like it: 'Love your neighbor as yourself.' All the Law and the Prophets hang on these two commandments." If we love God, he expects us to love everyone else. There are lots of different kinds of fruit, but they're all fruits that God created. There are lots of different types of people, but they're all created by God.

Ask→ • When Jesus is referring to loving our neighbor, who does he want us to love?

• In the movie the coach tells his players that they don't have to love each other, but they do have to respect each other. Why does God expect more from us?

• How does loving God with all our heart help us to love our neighbor?

THE CRUCIFIXION

Scripture: Matthew 27:32-56

Use this clip to discuss freedom.

The Critics Say

Movie Title:
SPIRIT (G)

Start Time: 15 minutes

Where to Begin: Spirit turns around and sees the soldiers right behind him. He whinnies to the other horses, and they run away.

Where to End: Spirit is led to the fort, and the officer says, "This one will be no different."

Plot: A wild horse, Spirit, is caught by soldiers and taken to a fort where the soldiers will try to "break" him.

Review: Use this scene to help kids understand the hopelessness Jesus' followers must have felt as they watched him be led away and crucified. The experience children have in this activity is sad but can help them grasp the reality of Jesus' death and the pain that he suffered for them.

NOW PLAYING

Say→ In this scene from *Spirit,* Spirit is captured.

Play the clip.

Ask→ • How do you think Spirit was feeling during this time?

• How do you think his family was feeling?

Say→ Spirit and his family felt very sad as he was led away to captivity, just as Jesus' disciples felt very sad as he was led to Calvary and crucified. Let's explore this a bit more.

Have students get comfortable sitting or lying on the floor, and tell them to close their eyes.

Say→ I'd like for you to travel with me in your imaginations to that awful day. You're in a crushing crowd of people, all moving toward a hill outside of town. You hear people screaming, yelling, and crying. Then you see the focus of their attention. It's Jesus, your Savior and friend, carrying a heavy beam of wood. He looks tired and sad, and you can tell the beam is much too heavy for him. But he keeps walking, even as people around him spit at him and laugh in his face. All too soon, the crowd reaches its destination. Soldiers force Jesus to the ground, and soon you hear the sickening thuds of heavy hammers, nailing Jesus' hands and feet to the cross. You see him raised into the air on that cross, and you raise your hands to him, crying and wishing you could do something to take him from the cross. He's not supposed to die...what about everything he promised you? Didn't he say he would be with you always? How can he be with you if he dies such a horrible death on a cross? You fall to your knees and sob.

Pause.

Say→ It's hard for us to imagine what it must have felt like to watch Jesus being crucified. The sadness must have been nearly unbearable. The good news is that Jesus didn't stay on that cross, and he didn't stay dead. He came back to life!

THE PARALYTIC IS HEALED

Scripture: Mark 2:1-5

Movie Title:
BALTO (G)

Use this clip to discuss possessing a strong faith in God during difficult times or Jesus' healing powers.

The Critics Say

Start Time: 34 minutes

Where to Begin: Balto watches as the town carpenter builds small coffins for the imminent deaths of the young children with diphtheria.

Where to End: Jenna gazes at Rosie through the window of the hospital, then turns and says "Balto" as she sees him heading out to retrieve the much-needed medicine.

Plot: Balto and a team of sled dogs race against time to bring back medicine to combat a serious diphtheria epidemic spreading among the children of Nome.

Review: Balto and his friends set out in the bitter cold to retrieve medicine for their friend Rosie and other ill children. The team battle various obstacles along the way but are persistent in their efforts. The paralytic's friends are just as persistent in getting their friend to Jesus to be healed. Use this clip to talk about the value of good friendships.

Supplies: Balloons, permanent markers, towels, and masking tape

Preshow: Use masking tape to establish a starting line and finishing line for the relay.

now PLAYING

Form groups of four. Have the children work together to inflate the balloon and add facial features with the marker. (Remind the children not to get the marker on their clothes and not to touch the marker on the balloon until it is completely dry.)

Have the children place the balloon person on an outstretched towel.

Say→ We're going to pretend that this balloon person is a friend, a very sick friend. First let's watch a movie clip about someone else who is very sick.

Show the *Balto* clip.

Ask→ • What happened to the children in this movie?

• How do you think the dog, Jenna, felt about her master, Rosie?

• How did Balto and the other animals feel about one another?

• Do you have a special friend who you would like to tell us about?

Say→ Good friends are wonderful. It's really fun to have friends to love and who love us. In the Bible there's a story about a man who couldn't walk. He was a paralytic. This man had some very good friends who loved him very much and whom he loved dearly. The friends loved him so much, that they did some special things to get him healed. The friends heard that Jesus was in town. They had heard stories about the wonderful healing powers of Jesus. The friends carried their friend on a mat to see Jesus, in hopes that he would heal the friend. But the home where Jesus was talking was so crowded that they couldn't get the friend's mat in the door. The friends had a great idea! They took the roof off the home and used ropes to lower their friend's mat into the house to see Jesus. Jesus healed the man. Now he could walk!

Ask→ • How do you think the man felt when Jesus healed him?

• How do you think the friends felt when their good friend was healed?

Say→ I'm sure the friends were happy that their friend could now walk! Let's play a game to help us remember our story. Remember the balloon man that we made? We're going to pretend he's the lame man resting on his mat. We're going to have a relay to see who can get him across the finish line first. Now, if your balloon man falls off, you'll have to go back to the starting line and start all over again!

Have the children stand in their groups of four. Let each person hold one corner of the towel with the balloon resting in the middle. On "Go," have the teams race to the finish line, starting over if the balloon falls off. Play several times, and see if children can improve their own times. Then mix the teams and play again as time allows.

JESUS CALMS THE SEA

Scripture: Mark 4:35-41

 Movie Title:
BEAUTY AND THE BEAST (G)

You can also use this clip to discuss being polite.

Start Time: 34 minutes

Where to Begin: The Beast is pacing back and forth and then says, "What's taking her so long?"

Where to End: Cogsworth says, "Well, we might as well go downstairs and start cleaning up."

Plot: The Beast wants Belle to join him for dinner but has trouble controlling his temper.

Review: The Beast has trouble controlling his temper, and those who care about him do what they can to encourage him, but his emotions are beyond their control. The storm that the disciples were afraid of was beyond their control as well. Use this clip to help children understand that only Jesus is always in control.

Supplies: Balloon, newsprint, marker, and tape

Preshow: Draw several bull's-eye type targets on the newsprint, and tape them around the room on the walls and floor.

NOW PLAYING

Have children stand close together in the center of the room.

Say→ When I say "go," choose a target to stand by what you think my balloon will hit when I let it go.

Blow up the balloon and let it go, causing it to fly around the room.

Ask→ • Was anyone successful at choosing the correct target?

• Why was it so difficult to choose the target you thought the balloon would hit or land on?

Say→ Let's play again. This time I want you to shout at the balloon to get it to do what you want it to.

Blow up the balloon again and let it go.

Ask→ • Did shouting at the balloon help?

• Is there anything you can do to control where the balloon goes each and every time?

Say→ We are going to watch a movie clip from *Beauty and the Beast.* The Beast's friends are trying to get him to control his temper. Let's watch and see what happens.

Show the *Beauty and the Beast* clip.

Ask→ • Why did the friends have such a hard time controlling the Beast's temper?

• Were any of them successful at making him do what he should do?

Say→ In the Bible there is a story about a terrible storm. The disciples and Jesus are in a boat, and the disciples are terribly afraid.

> Tell the Bible story from Mark 4:35-41.

Ask→ • What needed to be controlled in this story?

• Why couldn't the disciples control the storm?

• How were the disciples and the Beast's friends alike? different?

• Why could Jesus control the storm?

Say→ There is no way we can control a balloon, another person's temper, or a storm, but we don't have to because Jesus has all things under control.

JESUS BLESSES CHILDREN

Scripture: Mark 10:13-16

Movie Title:
A BUG'S LIFE (G)

You can also use this clip to teach children about friendship and teamwork.

Start Time: 41 minutes, 20 seconds

Where to Begin: Dot says, "Come on wings!" then falls and hangs onto the dandelion seed.

Where to End: The bugs escape into the thorn bush.

Plot: Dot, the smallest ant, is in trouble—her wings don't work well yet, and she has fallen from a dandelion. A hungry bird spies her and envisions lunch. The other bugs go through many obstacles to finally rescue Dot from the bird.

Review: Children may feel unimportant in a world where things are bigger than they are, and everyone is waiting for them to grow up. Use this scene to help kids realize that no matter how small or helpless they may feel, God feels that they are very important, and he can use them to do big things.

Supplies: Construction paper, markers, and tape

NOW PLAYING

Say→ I'd like to show you a scene from *A Bug's Life.* In this scene Dot, the smallest ant, is in danger of being eaten by a hungry bird.

> Play the clip.

Ask→ • Have you ever done something big that you didn't think you could do? How did you feel about that?

Say→ The bugs were much smaller and weaker than the bird, but they managed to rescue Dot. The bugs were very important; if they hadn't been there, Dot surely would have been eaten. Jesus thinks each of you is very important and special, too. In fact the Bible tells about a time that adults tried to keep children away from Jesus, but Jesus wanted the children to come close to him! Even if you feel as though you're too small to make a difference, Jesus has a special job for each of you. Let's learn more about our gifts and talents.

Give each student a sheet of construction paper, and have students write their names at the tops of the papers. Then have them tape the sheets around the room. Explain that you'd like students to circulate around to each other's papers and write about qualities or talents they see in each other. For example, someone might write "You're always patient" or "You're really good at speaking in front of other people." Encourage students to maintain a prayerful attitude while they do this. When students are finished, have them return to their own papers and read what others wrote. Then encourage them to think of ways they might use those gifts and talents in their lives to glorify God.

JESUS' BIRTH

Scripture: Luke 2:1-20

Movie Title:
TARZAN (1999) (G)

> The Critics Say
>
> Use this clip to discuss the fact that God keeps his promises, and he sent his only Son to be our Savior.

Start Time: 9 minutes

Where to Begin: As the male gorilla approaches, Terk hands the baby to Kala and says, "Her's going to be its mother now."

Where to End: The song ends, and Tarzan and the mother gorilla go to sleep.

Plot: A mother gorilla's baby is killed by a tiger, so the saddened gorilla adopts an orphaned human baby as her own. Tarzan becomes a very special and treasured baby to the gorilla mother.

Review: During the clip, the mother gorilla sings, "You'll be in my heart from this day on, now and forever more." From the moment of Jesus' birth, Mary must have had those same feelings. And when we accept Jesus into our hearts, we have Jesus with us always.

Supplies: Cardboard, scissors, red and white construction paper, paper, markers, and tape

Preshow: Cut a large heart shape from the cardboard. This will be used as a pattern by the children.

NOW PLAYING

Say→ When we treasure something, it becomes very special to us. We might say it takes a very special place in our heart. Let's watch a clip from *Tarzan* and see just what becomes very special to a gorilla.

> Show the *Tarzan* clip.

Ask→ • Why was Tarzan so special to this gorilla?

• How is that like you being special to your mom or dad?

• How is that also like Jesus being special to his mother, Mary?

Say→ When we read about Jesus' birth, we realize that Jesus was a very special baby. He was special to his mother, but he's even more special because Jesus is God's one and only Son. God sent Jesus to earth to die for our sins. That very special baby would grow to be the man who would give us life eternal.

> Have each child use the heart pattern to trace and cut a heart shape from red construction paper. Then have each child cut a pocket from white construction paper and tape it in place on the heart. Then have the children write names of people who are special and important to them on smaller slips of paper. Have kids place the strips in the pocket. Remind them that the things that are important to us are "in our heart" just like the song in today's movie.

Ask→ • How can you show these people how much you love them?

JESUS IS BAPTIZED (1)

Scripture: Luke 3:21-22

 Movie Title:
THE PRINCESS DIARIES (G)

> You can use this lesson to help children understand that when we accept Christ, we become new creations.

Start Time: 36 minutes, 50 seconds

Where to Begin: Mia rushes into the building, and her grandmother says, "You're late."

Where to End: The Queen looks at the transformed Mia and says, "Better. Much better."

Plot: Mia has recently learned she is the heir to the throne of Genovia. Her grandmother, the reigning queen, feels she needs a makeover to help her look more like a princess.

Review: Having the makeover pleases Mia's grandmother as it demonstrates the change from a plain schoolgirl into a real princess. This scene can help children understand that by being baptized, Jesus demonstrated that he was God's Son.

Supplies: Unpopped popcorn, disposable cups, air popper, and large bowl

> Be sure the children understand that when we are baptized there is no physical change, just a change in our hearts.
>
> *The Critics Say*

now playing

Have the children sit in a circle.

Put a few kernels of popcorn in a cup.

Pass the cup around for the children to touch and feel the kernels.

Ask➜ • Would anyone like to eat this popcorn the way it is?

Say➜ Of course not! We could eat it like this, but it wouldn't be very good and might even break our teeth. We need to pop it so it can be eaten. Let's do that.

Let the children watch as you pop the popcorn in the air popper into the large bowl. As it pops, comment on the physical change the popcorn goes through as it is being popped. Pass out the popcorn in cups for the children to eat as you watch your movie clip.

⚠ Allergy ALERT

Say➜ We're going to watch a scene from *The Princess Diaries*. Mia has recently learned she is a princess, the only heir to the throne of Genovia. Her grandmother would like for her to look more like a princess. Let's watch.

Show the clip.

Ask➜ • How do you think Mia felt about her new look?

• Was she still the same person as before? Why or why not?

Say➜ When Jesus was baptized by John the Baptist, it didn't change his physical appearance. But God was pleased with him as Jesus set an example for the rest of us to show the world that we have given our hearts to God.

Ask➜ • How do you think God feels when someone decides to give their life to him?

• How can you give your life to God?

JESUS IS BAPTIZED (2)

Scripture: Luke 3:21-22

Movie Title:
CHARLOTTE'S WEB (G)

> Use this clip to discuss sharing good news—especially the good news of God's love.
>
> *The Critics Say*

Start Time: 40 minutes

Where to Begin: The scene begins with "Some Pig" written in Charlotte's web.

Where to End: The newspapers blow away.

Plot: Wilbur knows he will be served as Christmas dinner without a miracle. His friend, Charlotte, spins the words "Some Pig" into her web.

This astonishes all who see it, and they begin to view Wilbur differently.

Review: When Jesus was baptized, God identified him as his Son. Use this clip to help children understand how names can shape lives.

Supplies: Baby name books

now Playing

Ask if any children know the meaning of their names. Have those who do share the meanings.

Ask→ • Why do you think names are important?

Say→ In this scene from *Charlotte's Web,* Charlotte spins the words *Some Pig* into her web in an effort to convince the Zuckermans that Wilbur is a special pig who should not be slaughtered.

Play the clip.

Ask→ • What would you think if you saw words like this spun into a spider's web?

• How do you think people started to view Wilbur after seeing these words?

Say→ In this clip we see how important a name is. What someone is called can change the way other people view him or her. In the Bible, Jesus was given a special name by God. When John the Baptist baptized Jesus, a form in the shape of a dove came from the sky, and all the people around heard God's voice saying, "This is my Son." This name caused many people to follow Jesus.

Your name is very important, too. Your parents chose your name because it meant something to them. Maybe you were named for a relative, or maybe your name reminds your parents of a special place or event.

Help children look up their names in the name books and share these with the class.

Say→ People might also be called by names other than their actual given names. Some of these names can be positive ones, while others might be kind of negative.

Ask→ • Are there any other names you're called?

• How does it make you feel when people call you names other than your given name?

Say→ No matter how many names we are called, there's one name that we are called that is the most important one—even more important than our given names. That name comes directly from God when he calls us "my son" or "my daughter." We are the children of God, and this name means more than any other.

JESUS CALLS FOLLOWERS

Scripture: Luke 5:1-11

Movie Title:
TOY STORY (G)

The Critics Say

You can use this scene to teach kids about loyalty, friendship, and helping others.

Start Time: 1 hour, 27 seconds

Where to Begin: Sid's alarm goes off.

Where to End: The toys gather around Woody, and he says, "It'll help everybody."

Plot: Toys Woody and Buzz end up in the room of Sid, the sadistic boy next door. As Sid plans to blow up Buzz with a rocket, Woody pleads with the toys in Sid's room to help him save Buzz.

Review: You can use this clip to remind kids of how Jesus called his disciples. Just as the toys all mobilized behind Andy to help him accomplish his mission, the disciples followed Jesus when he called. The toys set out to rescue and save Buzz from the dangerous situation he was in. Jesus came to save us from our dangerous and desperate situation of sin. Without Jesus, there is no hope of redemption, forgiveness, or freedom.

Supplies: Confetti and comb

NOW PLAYING

Say→ We're going to watch a scene from the movie *Toy Story*. In this part of the movie, Woody is asking the toys in Sid's room to help him rescue Buzz. Let's watch!

Play the movie clip.

Ask→ • Why did Woody ask the toys to follow him?

• What was unusual about the toys he asked for help?

• How did the toys respond?

Say→ In this scene the toys in Sid's room were ready to follow Andy and help him accomplish his mission. They responded when Andy called.

That reminds me of a story in the Bible about Jesus and his friends. When Jesus first began his ministry, he called people to follow him. And they did. These people weren't rich or powerful people—they were just regular, everyday people. But they left everything behind and followed Jesus because they knew that following Jesus is the most important thing anyone can ever do. They jumped to follow Jesus! Let's do a little experiment to show us what that might have been like.

Spread a small pile of confetti out on a table. Create static electricity on a comb by running it through your hair several times. Then hold the comb about an inch above the confetti, and watch the confetti jump up to the comb. Let children experiment with the confetti and comb too.

Say→ This confetti jumped right up to the comb, just as Jesus' followers left everything and jumped to follow Jesus. You know, Jesus is still calling people to follow him today. How can you follow Jesus?

THE GOOD SAMARITAN

Scripture: Luke 10:25-37

Movie Title:
🎥 **HOME ALONE (PG)**

Scene 1 Start Time: 5 minutes, 45 seconds

Be sure to start the tape for the Scene 1 start time at the point where the boys are going to the window. In the scene just prior to this, the older brother uses some inappropriate language.

Where to Begin: The boys look out the window, and one asks, "Who's he?"

Where to End: The old man looks up at the window where the boys are standing, and they quickly close the curtains.

Scene 2 Start Time: 1 hour, 29 minutes

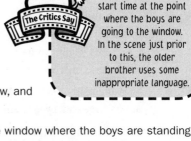

You can also use this clip to teach about gossip.

Where to Begin: The burglars open the door to the basement to find Kevin starting up the stairs.

Where to End: The old man rescues Kevin and carries him outside.

Plot: Due to neighborhood myths, Kevin is afraid of the man next door. Then Kevin is left home alone at Christmas, and two burglars break in. The burglars have him hanging on a door hook and are threatening to hurt him. He needs help.

Review: You can use this scene to help children understand that we shouldn't judge others. We may find a friend in someone unexpectedly.

Supplies: Construction paper, old magazines, scissors, glue sticks, and pens

NOW PLAYING

Have each child create a "neighborhood" by cutting out pictures of houses from the magazines and gluing them to the piece of construction paper. Ask children to think of imaginary people who might live in each of the houses in their neighborhood, such as a doctor, grocery store clerk, retired person, someone with lots of kids, and so on.

Ask→ • What is a neighbor?

• Who would be the best neighbor?

• Who would be a bad neighbor?

Say→ We're going to watch two scenes from *Home Alone.* In the first scene we hear Kevin's older brother describe the man who lives next door. Then Kevin learns the truth about the man.

Show the *Home Alone* clips.

Ask→ • Why do you think the boys were so willing to believe what Kevin's brother had to say about the old man?

• How do you think Kevin felt when the old man rescued him from the burglars?

Say→ The Bible tells about a man who asked Jesus "Who is my neighbor?" Jesus told the parable of the Good Samaritan. In this story a man was hurt, and the only one willing to help him was a supposed enemy. This story demonstrated that the true neighbor was the person who had mercy.

Ask→ • After learning about the Good Samaritan, what kind of neighbors would you like to have living near you?

• How can you be a good neighbor?

MARY AND MARTHA

Scripture: Luke 10:38-42

Movie Title:
THE MUPPET MOVIE (G)

You can also use this clip to discuss knowing what's important.

The Critics Say

Start Time: 1 hour, 12 minutes

Where to Begin: The Muppets are sitting around a campfire, and Gonzo has just finished singing a song.

Where to End: A falling star crosses the sky, and harmonica music begins.

Plot: Kermit and friends are trying to get to Hollywood, but because their car breaks down, they'll miss their audition. They're sitting around the campfire when Kermit realizes that focusing on disappointment and how he let down his friends is not important. What's important is that he listens to his heart and realizes what he promised himself.

Review: The Muppets are focused on disappointment. To them the only thing that's important is getting to Hollywood. Like Martha, they are focused on the wrong thing. Kermit realizes that being famous is not as important as being true to the promises he made himself.

Supplies: Bible, white socks, and permanent markers

NOW PLAYING

Hand out socks and markers.

Say→ Let's make a quick puppet! Draw a face on your sock so that when you put the sock on your hand, the face shows on top of the sock as you bend your wrist over.

Give kids a chance to draw faces on their socks. Ask kids to come up with names for their puppets. Then have kids introduce their puppets to partners and tell one thing their puppets want to do when they grow up.

Say→ Wow! Those are all very important things your puppets want to do! And they can spend their entire lives making sure they do those things. But there may just be something that's even more important than being a firefighter, or a singer, or a doctor.

In this movie the Muppets think the most important thing is getting to Hollywood to become famous. But the car breaks down, and everyone is sure they aren't going to make it in time for their big audition. Then Kermit realizes something that's even more important than the audition. Let's see if you can figure out what that is.

Show the *Muppet Movie* clip.

Ask→ • What do you think Kermit realized was most important?

• Why did talking to himself help him realize that?

• What was Kermit focused on before he talked to himself?

• What's most important to you?

• How do you know what's important to you?

Read aloud Luke 10:38-42.

Ask→ • Why is what Mary's doing more important?

• How can keeping your relationship with Jesus strong help you with what's most important?

Close by having kids sit quietly. Have them first think about the things during the day that keep them busy. Encourage them to talk to Jesus about those things. Encourage them to ask Jesus how they can make him the most important thing in their lives. Challenge kids to try this quiet prayer each night at home for the next week.

THE LORD'S PRAYER

Scripture: Luke 11:1-4

Movie Title:
MONSTERS, INC. (G)

You can use this clip to discuss communication.

Start Time: 32 minutes

Where to Begin: Boo rubs her eyes, and Sulley says, "I think she's getting tired."

Where to End: Sulley leaves the room and closes the door.

Plot: Sulley and Mike have to care for a human child, and they're not sure what to do with her. They're terribly afraid of her and are having difficulty communicating with her.

Review: Communication can be a tricky thing between two people or between a monster and a child, as in this movie. One thing we never have to worry about though is difficult communication between God and us. Jesus gives us an exact model to use when communicating with God.

Supplies: Index cards and marker

Preshow: Before class write several simple nouns and verbs on index cards, using one word per card. You might choose words such as *jump, run, phone, book,* or *read*. You'll need one card for each child.

now PLAYING

Say→ We are going to watch a movie clip from *Monsters, Inc.* I want you to watch closely and see how Sulley and Boo communicate with each other.

Show the movie clip.

Ask→ • How did Boo explain to Sulley what she was afraid of?

• How did Sulley explain to Boo what he wanted her to do?

• Have you ever had a hard time communicating with someone?

Say→ Let's play a game and see how well you can communicate with one another without using words.

Give each child an opportunity to act out one of the words on the game cards that you prepared earlier while the others guess what the word is.

Ask→ • What's the most difficult thing about not being able to talk?

• How were your feelings similar to the ones Sulley and Boo might have been feeling? How were they different?

Say→ Have you ever felt like you couldn't talk to God? Jesus' disciples wondered how they could talk to God. They asked Jesus to teach them.

Read Luke 11:1-4 aloud, or have a child read it aloud.

Ask→ • How does this passage help us know how to communicate with God?

• What are things we should say to God?

Say→ When we talk to God, there are no tricks, gimmicks, or special words that we have to use. We can just open our mouths and speak what's on our hearts and minds. Or we can talk to God silently. God wants us to talk to him, and he is always ready to listen.

PARABLE OF THE LOST SHEEP

Scripture: Luke 15:1-7

Movie Title:
FINDING NEMO (G)

You can also use this clip to discuss helping others.

Start Time: 1 hour, 24 minutes

Where to Begin: Nemo swims beside a chain and calls, "Dad! Dad!" then notices Dory swimming above him.

Where to End: Marlin embraces Nemo.

Plot: Marlin is a single parent clown fish whose only son, Nemo, has been captured by a scuba diver. Because he loves his son so much, Marlin sets off into the ocean to find him. After many perilous adventures, Marlin is reunited with his son.

Review: Nemo is a child who longs to be with his father, and Marlin is a father whose love for his son compels him to overcome any obstacle. What a great identification with God our Father and his tireless pursuit of each one of his sheep (or fish!).

Supplies: Plastic eggs and individually wrapped candy.

Allergy ALERT

Preshow: Before children arrive fill the eggs with candy, and hide them around the room.

NOW PLAYING

Say→ I've hidden some eggs around the room that are filled with surprises. This is not an Easter egg hunt; it's a *candy* hunt. Go!

Let the kids scatter and find as many eggs as they can. Have them return the eggs to the center of the room, and when all the eggs have been found, distribute them evenly among the children.

Ask→ • What made you run so fast to find the eggs?

• How did you feel when you found your first egg?

Say→ Hunting for someone or something is often hard work. Have you ever seen your parents lose their keys? Did they have fun looking for them? I didn't think so! But you seemed to have a *great* time looking for these eggs, and I think I know why: *Candy!* You love candy!

In this movie there's a dad who's looking for something. But unlike all of you, he is not having a good time. He is worried, he is frustrated, he is tired, and every now and then he is grumpy. He is looking for his son.

Show the *Finding Nemo* clip.

Ask→ • Who was happiest, Marlin or Nemo? Why?

• Why do you think Marlin endured so much in trying to find Nemo?

Say➜ Marlin loved Nemo so much that he went looking for him. God loves you and me so much that he would search the whole world to find us. Jesus told a story like *Finding Nemo* only he titled it *Finding the Lost Sheep*.

Read Luke 15:1-7 aloud.

Say➜ Just as Marlin looked for Nemo, and just as you eagerly looked for the candy, Jesus is always searching for those who have gone astray. Jesus loves us more than any parent and even more than you love candy!

PARABLE OF THE LOST SON

Scripture: Luke 15:11-32

 Movie Title:
**LADY AND THE TRAMP II:
SCAMP'S ADVENTURE (G)**

Use this clip to talk about God's forgiveness, the love of family, and obedience.

Start Time: 1 hour, 1 minute

Where to Begin: The dogs run to the house, and Jim Dear says, "What's all the commotion?"

Where to End: Jim Dear is talked into keeping the new puppy and says, "Welcome to the family, Angel."

Plot: Scamp longs for adventure and freedom. He runs away from home and joins a gang of junkyard dogs. When his father saves him from being impounded by the dogcatcher, Scamp decides to return home to the family he loves and who loves him.

Review: Scamp's family fears he might be lost forever. The prodigal son's father quite possibly thought he would never see his son again either. Both Scamp's family and the prodigal son's father welcomed them home with open arms. In the same way, God welcomes us to return to him.

Supplies: Small, individually wrapped candies

Allergy ALERT

Preshow: Hide the candies in the room before children arrive.

NOW PLAYING

Say➜ I've lost a few things, and I think they're in this room. Can you help me find them?

Give the children a chance to search for the candy. Allow the children to help one another so that each child finds one piece.

Ask➜ • How do you think I felt about losing my candy?

• Have you ever lost something important or special? If so, what happened?

- **How did you feel?**

- **How did you feel when you found that item?**

Say➔ When we lose something very important to us, we become sad. We want to search and search until we find that item. Let's watch a movie clip about someone who gets lost from his family.

Show the movie clip.

Ask➔ • How do you think Scamp's family felt when he came home?

Say➔ This reminds me of a story from the Bible. Read Luke 15:11-32 or tell the story in your own words.

Ask➔ • How is this story like Scamp's story?

- **How much does the father in the story love his son?**

- **How much does God love us?**

- **How do you think God feels when we come home to him?**

ZACCHAEUS

Scripture: Luke 19:1-10

Movie Title:
THE SWAN PRINCESS III: MYSTERY OF THE ENCHANTED TREASURE (G)

The Critics Say

You can also use this clip to talk about how Jesus loves us despite our sins and about God's forgiveness.

Start Time: 50 minutes

Where to Begin: Puffer and Speedy are talking to a captured Wizzer, attempting to get him to lead them to evil Zelda's hideout.

Where to End: Wizzer tells Puffer and Speedy the evil plot of Zelda and says, "That felt good."

Plot: Zelda wants to attain the Forbidden Arts and in turn be able to rule the world. She enlists the aid of a bird named Wizzer. A puffin, Puffer, and a turtle, Speedy, show Wizzer the error of his ways, and he has a complete turnaround.

Review: Puffer and Speedy convince Wizzer to choose "the right side" and be good and honest. Wizzer feels very good about himself as a new, "good" person. Zacchaeus had similar feelings about himself when Jesus called him to be a follower. Zacchaeus repented, correcting his wicked ways and vowed to return money he took dishonestly. You can use this clip to remind the children that when God calls us, we want to do what is right.

now PLAYING

Say➜ Let's watch a clip from *The Swan Princess III*.

Show the clip.

Ask➜ • How did the bird feel about himself after he decided to "choose the right side" and be good instead of evil?

• Can you tell about a time you chose to do the right thing?

Say➜ God wants us to be on his side and do what's right. In the Bible, we read of a man named Zacchaeus.

Read the account of Zacchaeus from Luke 19:1-10, or have a child read the story.

Ask➜ • How do you think Zacchaeus felt about changing his ways?

• How does it feel to do what's right?

• How does it feel to do what's wrong?

Have children work in small groups of three or four to make up a rhyme or rap about Zacchaeus. Allow a few minutes for groups to work, then have them perform their creative work for the rest of the group. Applaud all efforts, and remind children that this story is a good reminder to us to make good choices.

A WIDOW GIVES ALL

Scripture: Luke 21:1-4

 Movie Title:
E.T.: THE EXTRA-TERRESTRIAL (PG)

This clip can be used to discuss longing for a family.

Start Time: 1 hour, 20 minutes

Where to Begin: Scientists are studying E.T. and Elliott. The mother says, "What's the matter with Elliott?"

Where to End: A scientist tells Elliott, "I'm glad he met you first."

Plot: The extraterrestrial, who has become very ill, has been detained by scientists. Elliott has a strange connection with E.T. and is sick, too. For a small boy who has nothing more than bags of candy and the ability to be a friend, Elliott gives more to E.T. than a roomful of scientists could ever give him.

Review: E.T. is the witness to a boy who offers unconditional love to a creature who wants nothing but to go home. While there are adults everywhere who can't seem to give E.T. what he needs, a young boy becomes his greatest hope and gives him everything, even risking his own health to do so. Similarly, the widow in Luke 21 has given almost everything she has. It's this unconditional generosity toward others that Jesus encourages in all of us.

 Supplies: Bag of candy such as M&M's or Reeses Pieces

NOW PLAYING

Hand out small handfuls of candy to each child, but vary the amount you give to them. Be sure that there are four or five kids who don't get any candy. Be sure also that several kids only have a few candies.

Say→ If you've ever seen the movie *E.T.,* you'll know that one of the ways Elliott connects with E.T. is with candy. That's how we'll connect with each other today. Some of you have candy, and some of you don't. Let's share.

Have kids share their candy and enjoy the treat.

Say→ That was awfully nice of you to give to others, even when some people may have had more candy than you. In our movie, Elliott was a very generous boy, too. He wanted to help E.T. find his home. And he did everything he could to help him. Let's watch.

Show the *E.T.* clip.

Ask→ • Why do you think the man was glad that E.T. met Elliott first?

• How do you think Elliott helped E.T.?

• Why did Elliott think he could help E.T. better than the doctors and scientists could?

Say→ We all have helped other people. And sometimes we may not feel like there's much we can do. Elliott was just a little boy. He was surrounded by adults who couldn't help E.T. Elliott was sick and still thought he was the best person to help E.T. find his home. God wants us to give it our best when we help others, even if it feels like we don't have a lot to give. Let's read a story about another person who gave a lot.

Read Luke 21:1-4.

Have pairs discuss these questions:

• Why did Jesus say the widow was more generous than those who gave more money?

• What do the widow and Elliott from *E.T.* have in common?

• Can you think of any other people who give everything to help others?

PETER DENIES JESUS

Scripture: Luke 22:54-62

 Movie Title:
A WALK TO REMEMBER (PG)

Use this clip to teach kids about hurt feelings.

Start Time: 29 minutes, 39 seconds

Where to Begin: In the hall at school, Carter's friend says, "Here comes your leading lady."

Where to End: Carter and Jamie are at Jamie's home, talking on the porch. Stop immediately after Jamie says, "I was very wrong" since there is a bad word immediately following that scene.

Plot: A boy popular with the cool crowd needs help from Jamie, a pastor's daughter. They begin to like each other, but the cool kid, Carter, reveals his own shallowness by betraying their budding friendship when he's around his friends.

Review: Just as Peter betrayed Jesus, Carter betrays his friendship with Jamie. This clip helps children identify with the feelings associated with peer pressure and betrayal.

 Supplies: One shoelace per child

now PLAYING

Ask→ • What does it feel like when someone talks bad about you to someone else?

• What does it feel like when a close friend is the one doing the talking?

Say→ Friends are supposed to be loyal and stick up when other people talk bad about us. But even good friends can often slip up whether unintentionally or in a weak moment of peer pressure. Carter is a popular kid in school, and Jamie isn't. But through a variety of circumstances, they become friends. Then one day Carter is with his cool friends, and he betrays Jamie. Let's see what happens.

Show the movie clip.

Ask→ • Why would Carter do this to Jamie?

• How do you think Jamie felt?

Say→ Fortunately, in the movie, Carter and Jamie find a way to apologize and receive forgiveness. A similar event happened in the Bible, and this time it wasn't just a story—it was for real. Peter betrayed his best friend Jesus at a very weak moment.

Read Luke 22:54-62 aloud, or paraphrase the events.

Ask→ • Why do you think Peter betrayed Jesus?

• How do you think Peter felt later?

Say→ Fortunately, for Peter, Jesus was able to forgive him.

Ask→ • How do you think Peter felt when he found out Jesus would forgive him?

Say→ We know there will be times when close friends will betray us or say something mean to hurt our feelings. But we also have the power to forgive them.

Give each child a shoelace.

Say→ This shoelace represents our good friends; notice how nice and smooth things are. But when we hurt people's feelings or betray them we place a knot in our relationship.

Have each child tie a knot in his or her shoelace.

Ask→ • How can we deal with this knot?

• How can we deal with the knots in our friendships?

Say→ We can get upset about knots in our friendships, we can throw a friendship away, or we can forgive our friends and untie the knots. The best choice is to treat our friends the way we would want to be treated, even if they sometimes don't remember to treat us this way.

JESUS TURNS WATER INTO WINE (1)

Scripture: John 2:1-12

You can also use this clip to discuss miracles.

The Critics Say

Movie Title:
CINDERELLA (1997) (NOT RATED)

Start Time: 36 minutes

Where to Begin: Cinderella is sitting in her rocking chair and says, "I guess I know what you're gonna say."

Where to End: Cinderella hugs her godmother and says, "Thank you Godmother!"

Plot: In this version of the classic Rodgers and Hammerstein musical, Cinderella longs to go to the ball and dance with the prince. When her fairy godmother shows up and flourishes her magic wand, Cinderella's life is suddenly changed.

Review: The fairy godmother could change mice into men and a pumpkin into a carriage, but only Jesus truly changed water into wine. Use this clip to remind children of the transforming power that belongs to God.

Supplies: Dress-up clothing with accessories and two large boxes

Preshow: Divide the clothing and accessories between the two boxes. Set the boxes several feet away from each other at one end of the room.

NOW PLAYING

Say→ I'd like to show you a scene from *Cinderella.* Let's see what happens.

Play the clip.

Ask→ • What was Cinderella's dream?

- **Why did some things need to be transformed to make Cinderella's dream come true?**

Say→ In this clip Cinderella and many of the things in her home were transformed. While this transformation was just a pretend story, there's an account of another kind of transformation in the Bible that was a true miracle.

Read John 2:1-12 aloud, or have a volunteer read it.

Ask→ • What was transformed in this story?

• Why do you think Jesus did this?

• What would you have thought if you had been a guest at this wedding?

Say→ Let's play a game to remind us of the miraculous, transforming power of God. It's called Transformation Tag.

Have students form two equal teams, and have each team line up on the opposite side of the room from the boxes. Have each team choose a "Transformer." Have the Transformers stand beside the boxes.

Say→ These are the "before" pictures. You see how these two look now; let's see what they look like after their teams transform them!

Have the first person in each line run up to the box, choose an item, put it on the Transformer, then run back to the team. The second person on the team will do the same thing until all the children have had a turn or until all the dress-up items have been used. Then have the Transformers stand so everyone can see them.

Choose children who will not be easily embarrassed to be your Transformers.

Give a round of applause for both teams and their Transformers.

Say→ It's fun to see the changes that take place in this game, but only God can do a transforming miracle!

JESUS TURNS WATER INTO WINE (2)

Scripture: John 2:1-12

You can also use this scene to help the children understand that God can use circumstances in our lives to prove his presence.

Movie Title:
BATTERIES NOT INCLUDED (PG)

Start Time: 33 minutes, 20 seconds

Where to Begin: Several neighbors are on the roof, and one says, "It could be giant rats." *Note that there's cursing just before this, so be sure to cue the beginning correctly.*

Where to End: Faye smiles at her neighbors as they look on in wonder at what they have just witnessed.

Plot: When Frank and his neighbors find Faye on the roof throwing nails and screws as if feeding the birds, they think she's gone mad. Then they see for themselves how the creatures can fix things after Faye smashes Frank's pocket watch, and the "little guys" put it back together in mere seconds.

Review: You can use this scene to help the children understand how the people in Jesus' time must have felt as they witnessed his miracles. When they witnessed with their own eyes the miracles he performed, they were convinced that he truly was the Son of God. We can have the confidence that Jesus is exactly who he claimed to be.

> The Critics Say
>
> Make sure your children realize that Jesus was not performing magic or illusions. It was truly God's power working through him.

Supplies: Index cards, scissors, markers, and envelopes

now playing

Have each child draw a colorful picture on an index card, then cut it into about eight pieces. Let children exchange envelopes and put together the puzzles. Then have children put their pieces into an envelope and set them aside.

Ask→
- **How hard or easy was it to complete these puzzles?**
- **If someone could put together a puzzle quickly would you think it was a miracle?**

Say→ We're going to watch a scene from *Batteries Not Included*. Frank finds his wife on the roof of their apartment building. She has discovered some little creatures who can do some miraculous things, but Frank and the neighbors don't believe her.

Show the clip from *Batteries Not Included*.

Ask→
- **How do you think Faye felt when no one believed her?**
- **How do you think she felt when everyone realized what was happening?**

Say→ Faye knew these little creatures could do miraculous things, but no one would believe her. Until they saw with their own eyes, they didn't believe her. The little creatures were able to put together the pieces of a watch, and it seemed like a miracle. Putting together a puzzle isn't really a miracle, but it does take practice. The Bible tells us about a time Jesus turned water into wine.

Retell the account from John 2:1-12.

Say→ While we can figure out puzzles, and the creatures in the movie could solve puzzles with incredible speed, only Jesus can do true miracles.

JESUS TALKS WITH A SAMARITAN WOMAN

Scripture: John 4:1-26

Movie Title:
TO KILL A MOCKINGBIRD (NOT RATED)

The Critics Say

Use this clip to discuss gossip.

Start Time: 8 minutes, 54 seconds

Where to Begin: Jem says, "There goes the meanest man that ever took a breath of life."

Where to End: Jem says, "And he drools most of the time."

Plot: Scout and Jem, the children of small-town lawyer Atticus Finch, are afraid of their mostly unseen neighbor Boo Radley.

Review: Jesus demonstrated his own lack of prejudice with his words and actions to the Samaritan woman. This movie clip helps children see the damage done by prejudice, and the hurt that it causes.

NOW PLAYING

Assign each child a number. Explain that you're going to play Tag. When you call out a number, the person with that number becomes "It" and must chase the others. Those who are tagged freeze in place. But every minute or so, you'll call out a new number. When you call out a new number, everyone who is frozen immediately becomes unfrozen, and the person who has the number you called becomes the new "It." Play for several minutes, calling out new numbers randomly and as often as you like. Then have children sit down.

Ask➔ • How does it feel to be "It"?

• How would you feel if everyone always ran away from you in real life?

• Why do we sometimes treat people like that?

Say➔ In the movie *To Kill a Mockingbird,* Jem and Scout are a brother and sister who meet a new boy in town. They tell him about a man in their neighborhood.

Show the *To Kill a Mockingbird* clip.

Ask➔ • From what Jem describes, what kind of person do you expect to meet?

Say➔ Boo Radley, Jem and Scout's neighbor, ends up saving Scout's life, and Scout learns a valuable lesson on forming an opinion about someone before you have all the facts in. We get our word *prejudice* from pre-judge—to form an opinion before you know for sure. In the Bible the Jews hated the Samaritans, who they felt were not pure or good. They had prejudice against them. Notice what Jesus, who was himself a Jew, did to this woman he met.

Retell the account from John 4:1-26.

Ask→ • Why do you think Jesus treated this woman with kindness, even though everyone else kept away from her?

• What can we learn from Jesus' example?

JESUS RAISES LAZARUS

Scripture: John 11:1-44

Movie Title:
THE SECRET GARDEN (1993)

You can also use this clip to teach children about the wonders of creation.

The Critics Say

Start Time: 1 hour, 6 minutes

Where to Begin: Mary and Dickon wheel Colin to the secret garden for the first time, and Colin asks, "Are these your animals?"

Where to End: Colin is petting a baby deer and says, "I'm going to come here tomorrow."

Plot: Mary's cousin, Colin, has been bedridden with a series of perceived illnesses. Mary convinces Colin to experience the outdoors and to visit a hidden, secret garden. The garden becomes a special place of friendship and physical and emotional healing.

Review: Use this clip to teach children about the miracle of Jesus raising Lazarus from the dead. Give the kids the opportunity to think about how Lazarus must have felt when he realized he was alive and saw the world knowing that he had been dead for four days, and compare this to Colin's realization that he could enjoy life after all.

Supplies: Adding machine tape or toilet paper

Preshow: Prior to class darken the room as much as possible. Have the lights turned off and the windows covered.

NOW PLAYING

Have children form small groups. Give each group a roll of adding machine tape or toilet paper. Tell the children to wrap one child in the tape or paper as if these were burial clothes. Have the wrapped children stand as still as possible, and have the others remain quiet as if they were mourning the loss of a friend.

Say→ I'm going to read John 11:41-44 from the Bible. When you hear me say "Lazarus come out." I want those wrapped in paper to stand up and break free of the your imaginary grave clothes, and everyone else can cheer.

Read the passage.

Say→ We're going to watch a scene from *The Secret Garden*. In this scene we're going to see Colin, a boy who hasn't been able to get out of bed for many years, experience going outside for the first time.

Show *The Secret Garden* clip.

Ask→ • What would Colin have seen, smelled, and felt for the first time when he went outside?

• How was Colin's experience like Lazarus being raised from the grave by Jesus?

• Do you think Lazarus and Colin would have a new appreciation for life after their experiences? Why or why not?

Say→ Mary, Martha, and Jesus loved Lazarus very much. The Bible says that when Jesus saw the tomb where Lazarus was buried, he wept. In John 11:25 Jesus stated that he is the resurrection and the life. That means Jesus even has power over death.

JESUS WASHES FEET

Scripture: John 13:1-17

The Critics Say

You can also use this clip to discuss cheerfulness and willingness to do hard work.

Movie Title:
CINDERELLA II: DREAMS COME TRUE (G)

Start Time: 7 minutes, 21 seconds

Where to Begin: The clock chimes, and the castle comes into view and Prudence knocks on the door.

Where to End: Prudence says, "Just do as I say, and everything will be fine."

Plot: Cinderella must learn how to pursue life as a queen. She is not comfortable with her newfound regal status, and the comedy comes in when she tries to fumble with her old servant role.

Review: A queen-like Cinderella would not be expected to do chores, and we wouldn't expect Jesus, the Son of God, to humble himself and do menial tasks either. Use this clip to show children that Jesus served others and wants us to serve others too.

Supplies: Index cards and pen

Preshow: On each index card, write a menial task children would not want to do, such as clipping someone else's toenails, taking out the trash, or cleaning the litter box.

NOW PLAYING

Have children form groups of three or four. Give each group an index card, and allow children a few minutes to determine how they will act out this task. Then have each group pantomime their task for everyone else and see if the others can guess what they're doing.

Ask→ • **Would you ever do any of these tasks without being asked? Why or why not?**

• **What would motivate you to do them without being asked?**

Say→ In the movie *Cinderella II,* Cinderella has moved up the social ladder from a servant in a house where she was unloved to the position of queen. But old habits are hard to break.

Show the *Cinderella II* clip.

Ask→ • **Why do you think it was so hard for Cinderella to not do tasks that servants had been assigned?**

• **Why wasn't Cinderella asked to do these tasks?**

Say→ Cinderella never had to be asked to do these chores because it came naturally for her. She even sang while she did these jobs! She had the heart of a humble servant. Notice what Jesus did to teach this lesson to his disciples.

Read John 13:1-17.

Ask→ • **How were Jesus' actions like Cinderella's?**

• **Why were Jesus' actions so unexpected?**

• **Why was Peter so put out with Jesus for scrubbing his toes?**

• **What would you have done if you were there?**

Say→ Serving does not come easily unless we practice.

Ask→ • **What are acts of service you can do this week that will communicate with your family what a true servant of Jesus would do?**

JESUS IS THE WAY TO GOD

Scripture: John 14:6-10

 Movie Title:
LILO & STITCH (PG)

Use this clip to teach children about feeling rejected.

Start Time: 57 minutes, 18 seconds

Where to Begin: Stitch is crying in the woods.

Where to End: Stitch runs away from the alien.

Plot: Stitch is an escaped alien who longs to have a family. Aliens come to Earth to claim Stitch and destroy him.

Review: The movie illustrates the importance of belonging to a family and serves as a reminder that we all have a longing to belong to God.

Use this clip to demonstrate that we need Jesus to lead us to a relationship with God.

Supplies: Paper, tape, marker, index cards, and pencils

Preshow: Write the following questions on sheets of paper, one question per paper, and tape them around your room.

- What do you need to check out a library book?
- What do you need to see a movie in a theatre?
- What do you need to drive a car?
- What do you need to ride the subway or bus?
- What do you need to get into a locked house?
- What do you need to bake a pie?
- What do you need to catch a fish?

NOW PLAYING

Give each child several index cards and a pencil. Let children move around the room and answer as many questions as they have time for. To answer a question, kids should write their answers on an index card and leave it beside the paper with the matching question. After several minutes, gather the kids together, and read some of the answers from each of the question stations.

Say→ To do each of these tasks, we need something that will help us. It might be something like a key, a token, or a recipe, but it's some form of help. Let's watch a movie clip to see what this creature needs.

Show the clip.

Ask→ • What did Stitch long to have?

• What was Stitch told?

Say→ This clip reminds me of Jesus' disciples. They longed to be with Jesus and needed help and direction, too. Jesus had told them he was leaving them, and they were sad.

Read John 14:6-10.

Say→ Jesus said he is the way, the truth, and the life. He said he is the only way to God. Stitch needed someone to help him belong. When we have a relationship with Jesus, we belong to God!

THE RESURRECTION

Scripture: John 20:1-21

Movie Title:
SPIRIT (G)

Start Time: 1 hour, 5 minutes

Where to Begin: Spirit and the boy see soldiers. The boy yells, "Run!" as the soldiers begin to chase them.

Where to End: Spirit and the boy are riding together across the desert.

Plot: Spirit and the Indian have finally managed to escape the soldiers. They are running through the canyon when they come to a great ravine they must cross. Spirit runs, jumps, and lands safely on the other side.

Review: Jesus' followers had been through a frightening ordeal, just as Spirit and the boy had with the chase. When the boy and Spirit were free, they felt joy. Use this scene to help kids understand the amazing joy Jesus' followers felt when they realized he was alive— joy your students can share!

Supplies: Chenille wires

> You can also use this clip to discuss perseverance.

The Critics Say

NOW PLAYING

Say→ In this scene from *Spirit*, Spirit and the boy face a dangerous dilemma.

Play the clip.

Ask→ • How do you think Spirit and the boy felt when they realized they'd escaped?

• How did you feel as you watched this scene?

Say→ Spirit and the boy felt tremendous joy when they made it across the ravine and escaped. In the same way, Jesus' followers felt great joy when they realized their Savior and friend was not dead after all. He was alive, and he would live forever with them. What great news! Let's make some sculptures as we think about this turnaround from fear to great joy.

Give each student two or three chenille wires. Ask students to begin by sculpting the wires into symbols of the fear and sadness the disciples must have felt when Jesus was crucified. Then have them undo these sculptures and create symbols of the great joy the disciples must have felt when they realized Jesus was alive and with them forever. Give students time to share about their creations.

Say→ Spirit and the boy had reason to celebrate when they escaped the soldiers, and the disciples had reason to celebrate when Jesus escaped death. We can celebrate too!

JESUS RETURNS TO HEAVEN

Scripture: Acts 1:6-11

Use this movie to discuss giving gifts and encouraging others.

The Critics Say

Movie Title:
MONSTERS, INC. (G)

Start Time: 1 hour, 23 minutes, 18 seconds

Where to Begin: Mike says, "I'm on the cover of a magazine!" and the teeth start chattering on the floor.

Where to End: The girl's voice says, "Kitty!" and Sulley smiles.

Plot: Sulley and Mike are monsters who have fallen in love with a little girl. They've been separated from her for a long time and miss her a lot. Now Mike has found a way for them to be together again.

Review: The movie illustrates a simple lesson of friendship and fearless love. Though these two worlds are hidden from each other, they intersect in more ways than one. In the same way, our world here on earth is separated from the hidden world of heaven, and we spend our life here longing for the joy of seeing Jesus face to face.

 Supplies: Paper and pencils

NOW PLAYING

Have children form small groups, and provide them with paper and pencils. Explain that you want kids to think of things parents or teachers might say before they leave a room, such as "Everyone sit at their desks till I get back." These can be funny or serious things that adults really might say. Give children several minutes to discuss and write their answers, then have a volunteer from each group share their responses.

Ask➜ • **Do the things adults say make you want them to come back or not?**

• **What do you usually do while you're waiting? Do you obey or not?**

Say➜ **Jesus said goodbye to his followers when he left Earth and went to heaven. Let's read what happened.**

Read Acts 1:6-11 aloud.

Ask➜ • **What instructions did Jesus give?**

• **Do you know if the followers obeyed these instructions or not?**

• **How are you obeying these instructions?**

• **What do you think it will be like when we get to see Jesus face to face?**

Say➜ **Let's watch this clip from *Monsters, Inc.* Mike and Sulley love Boo but have been separated from her for a long time.**

Show the clip.

Ask→ • What do you think Mike, Sulley, and Boo were feeling in this movie?

• How are these feelings like ones we might have when we get to see Jesus face to face?

PENTECOST

Scripture: Acts 2:1-13

Movie Title:

THE FOX AND THE HOUND (G)

You can also use this clip to teach children about friendship such as the biblical account of Jonathan and David.

Start Time: 17 minutes, 35 seconds

Where to Begin: Copper, the hound dog, and Tod, the fox, meet for the first time at a hollowed out log.

Where to End: Tod and Copper begin playing hide and seek, and the owl says, "My, my. Look at that. A fox and a hound playing together."

Plot: Tod is an orphan fox being raised by a loving grandmother. Copper is a hound dog that will be trained to sniff out and find foxes for his master. The two meet in the woods and become best friends.

Review: In this clip animals who should be enemies come together in friendship. Use this example to help children understand the miracle at Pentecost, when people of all languages came together and were able to understand the message of God's love.

Supplies: Poster board and marker

Preshow: Write the following words for *thank you* on a poster board: thank you (English), merci (French), gracias (Spanish), arigatou (Japanese), grazie (Italian).

NOW PLAYING

Say→ We're going to watch a scene from *The Fox and the Hound*. In this scene Tod, the fox, and Copper, the hound dog, meet each other for the first time.

Show *The Fox and the Hound* clip.

Ask→ • Why is it unusual that a fox and a hound would become best friends?

• How do these animals overcome their differences?

Say→ The Bible tells about a time when people with different languages were able to overcome their differences through a miracle.

Retell the events recorded in Acts 2:1-13, or read this passage aloud.

Say→ God caused this to happen so that people who spoke different languages could all understand the message of God's love. Let's do an activity that will help us get an idea of what it might have been like there.

Show children the poster board, then teach the kids each language's way of saying thanks. Then have children form five groups, and assign each group a language. Explain that when you call out the language, such as French, those assigned that language should shout out "thank you" in that language. Start calling out the languages, getting faster and faster so that soon children are all calling out "thank you" at the same time.

Say➜ That's a lot of noise! Imagine being someplace where everyone was speaking different languages at the same time, and everyone wanted information from you. That would be overwhelming! That's what it might have been like for the disciples. It's wonderful that God allowed everyone to hear and understand the message of his love in the right language!

PETER AND JOHN BEFORE THE SANHEDRIN

Scripture: Acts 4:1-22

Movie Title:
JOE SOMEBODY (PG)

You can also use this scene to discuss bullies.

Start Time: 1 hour, 24 minutes, 31 seconds

Where to Begin: Joe has arrived at the playground for the big fight to regain his honor. Someone shouts, "There he is!"

Where to End: When Joe says, "It's OK."

Plot: Joe has been humiliated by the office bully and vows revenge. In this scene Joe finally gets his priorities straight and understands how to properly deal with the bully.

Review: Peter and John didn't back down when they stood before the Sanhedrin. In this movie clip, Joe doesn't back down either—but he doesn't fight. This scene demonstrates the courage it takes to do the right thing.

now PLAYING

Say➜ In this movie Joe has lost a fight with the office bully and has been training for a rematch. He wants to beat the bully. Everyone thinks Joe's a hero for preparing to fight, except for his daughter. She thinks he should just walk away. Let's watch and see who Joe listens to.

Show the *Joe Somebody* clip.

Ask➜ • What would you do if you were Joe?

• What do you think your friends would say if you backed down from a fight?

Say➜ Joe had a choice to make, and he chose wisely. While he wasn't the most popular guy, he was a hero to those who were closest to him. John and Peter were faced with a similar problem. As followers of Jesus, they were on trial for what they believed. They could have chosen not to say anything and be set free or stand up for what they believed and face the consequences that could have included death.

Read Acts 4:1-22.

Ask→ • Why were Peter and John so confident?

• What do you think Peter and John were feeling just before they began to speak?

Say→ Just as Peter and John stood up boldly for what they believed, so God calls you to stand up in front of your family, your friends, and classmates to not be ashamed of what you feel and think. It's hard to tell people where you go to church, what you pray about, or even what you believe God has done for you.

Ask→ • What will give you more confidence to share what you feel about Jesus to your friends?

Have children form pairs and practice telling each other about Jesus. Allow enough time for each child to share with the other. Explain that practicing can help us have more confidence and courage as we stand firm for Jesus. Close with prayer, asking God to give the children courage to share God's love.

PAUL SHIPWRECKED

Scripture: Acts 27:27-44

You can also use this scene to discuss helping others.

Movie Title:
SWISS FAMILY ROBINSON (G)

Start Time: 6 minutes

Where to Begin: The family is loading the raft, and the oldest brother says, "But I don't see how we can take all these animals."

Where to End: The family lands ashore, and the dogs jump off the raft.

Plot: On their way to New Guinea, the Robinson family encounters disaster, and they must make a new life on a deserted island.

Review: Just as the family in the movie, Paul also faced a shipwreck. Use this scene to help children understand that we can trust God at all times, even in times of great danger.

 Supplies: Paper, colorful tissue paper, and glue sticks

NOW PLAYING

Have children tear pieces of tissue paper and glue them to the paper to create a picture of a boat nearing shore. Don't allow kids to use other items such as pencils or scissors. Allow time for children to finish their crafts.

Ask→ • What made this project difficult?

     • What are other difficult situations you've had in your life?

     • How did you feel when you didn't know what to do?

     • Who was able to help you through that situation?

Say→ All of us face difficult situations. Let's see how this movie family handles one.

     Show the *Swiss Family Robinson* clip.

Ask→ • Who took care of the situation?

     • Who was watching over the animals?

Say→ Just as the animals were taken care of by the family, we are always watched over by God. There is a true story of a shipwreck in the Bible. Let's see how Paul and the other ship's passengers responded to their emergency.

     Read Acts 27:27-44.

Ask→ • How would you have felt if you were in Paul's place on that ship or in the water?

     • What made Paul so confident in the middle of such a difficult situation?

     • How can we have that same confidence?

BODY IMAGE

Scripture: Genesis 1:27

 Movie Title:
THE SANTA CLAUSE (PG)

You can also use this clip to teach children about concern for others.

Start Time: 57 minutes, 16 seconds

Where to Begin: Boss says, "I don't know what's happening to you."

Where to End: Doctor hears "Jingle Bells" playing through the stethoscope.

Plot: Scott, now serving as Santa Claus, is putting on extra weight as part of his new duties. He struggles to find a solution as everyone around him is concerned about the changes his body is going through.

Review: You can use this scene to help children understand body image and how God views us. We all tend to worry about how we look and what we can do to help us look better. The focus is on the outside and tends to give us a negative feeling. But, being created in the image of God, we need to realize that everything about us is by de-sign, and God loves us just the way we are.

Supplies: Aluminum foil

Preshow: As neatly as possible, tear enough sheets of foil off for each stu-dent to have a 12-inch square.

now PLAYING

Say→ We're going to watch a scene from *The Santa Clause*. Scott has taken on the responsibilities of being Santa Claus and is starting to change to look like Santa Claus. These changes are starting to worry Scott and the people around him. Let's watch.

Show the clip from *The Santa Clause*.

Ask→ • What would you think if your body changed the way we just saw in this movie clip?

• How would it make you feel?

Give each student a piece of aluminum foil.

Say→ Look at your image in the foil. Make an effort to see a clear image of your-self. Now smash the foil into a ball. Next I want you to try to spread the foil and look at your image again.

Ask→ • Which image of yourself do you prefer, the one before or after you smashed the foil? Why?

Say→ God sees us as his creations who are made in his image. Other people's comments about us being too tall or small or too heavy or thin can crumple us. Genesis 1:27 says, "So God created man in his own image, in the image of God he created him; male and female he created them."

Ask➔ • How do you feel knowing we are all created in the image of God?

• How should this affect the way we look at ourselves?

• How should this affect the way we look at others?

SELF-ESTEEM

Scripture: Joshua 1:9

Movie Title:
HOOSIERS (PG)

> *The Critics Say*
> You can also use this clip to teach children about trusting God and doing everything for the Lord.

Start Time: 1 hour, 24 minutes

Where to Begin: Ollie, player number 13 and the shortest player, is fouled as he takes a shot.

Where to End: Ollie is victoriously being carried off the court by his teammates.

Plot: Hickory High School is trying to win a state basketball championship against much larger schools. In a closely contested regional play-off game, Hickory High School has to rely on its shortest player, Ollie, to make two critical free throws. He's an underdog but comes through to win the game.

Review: Often children lack confidence in things they think they're not good at. Sometimes that lack of confidence leads to not trying new things. Show the children this video clip of a teenager who many thought was not big enough or athletic enough. Use Joshua 1:9 to help kids realize God is with them wherever they go, and they don't have to be afraid or discouraged to try in difficult circumstances.

Supplies: Trash can, masking tape, and two foam balls

Preshow: Prior to class time, set the trash can against a wall as the basketball bucket. Mark just a few feet away from the can a foul line using the masking tape.

NOW PLAYING

Give each child a chance to make two shots with the balls. Have them pretend they're playing basketball, and they're about to win the game with two free throws. Allow each child to shoot until they make two shots. If time permits let kids shoot the foul shots two more times.

Say➔ We're going to watch a scene from the movie *Hoosiers.* In the video clip we're going to watch Ollie, the shortest player on the team. Earlier in the movie, he had to make two free throws, and he missed.

Show the *Hoosiers* clip.

Ask➔ • How do you think Ollie felt as he stepped to the foul line to shoot the free throws?

- **How do you think he would have felt after making the free throws?**

Say→ Sometimes we don't think we have the ability to do something. We may think we're not good enough, or fast enough, or musical enough, or smart enough. But God wants us to try. Joshua 1:9 says, "Have I not commanded you? Be strong and courageous. Do not be terrified; do not be discouraged, for the Lord your God will be with you wherever you go." God will help us do things even if we don't feel like we can.

Ask→ • **Do you think Ollie felt good about himself as a person before the free throws? Why or why not?**

• **Do you think Ollie would have been a hero even if he had missed the free throws? Why or why not?**

• **How can Joshua 1:9 give you comfort in difficult times?**

NATURE

Scripture: Psalm 8

 *Movie Title:*
ALADDIN (G)

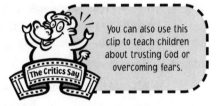
You can also use this clip to teach children about trusting God or overcoming fears.

Start Time: 57 minutes

Where to Begin: Aladdin says, "It's a magic carpet" and convinces Jasmine to take a ride.

Where to End: Aladdin and Jasmine finish the song, and fireworks burst.

Plot: Aladdin is trying to impress Jasmine because he likes her. He offers to take her on a magic carpet ride. She agrees, and the two of them see the beauty of the world from a new perspective.

Review: Sometimes we take God's creation for granted. In this clip Jasmine sees the world and its beauty from a different point of view. Use this clip to help kids have a greater appreciation of creation and thereby have a greater understanding of the Creator.

Supplies: Poster board and tape. *Note: Children will gather additional supplies outside.*

NOW PLAYING

Say→ We're going to watch a video clip from the movie *Aladdin.* In the scene we're going to see Aladdin taking Princess Jasmine on a magic carpet ride. Listen closely to the words of the song they're singing.

Show the *Aladdin* clip.

Ask→ • **How do you think it would feel to see the world from way up high on a magic carpet ride?**

• **What did Jasmine see that made her happy?**

Say→ We're going to take a walk outside. While we're outside everyone should find one item God made that's small enough to fit in one hand, such as a leaf, a blade of grass, or a dandelion.

Once outside give the children a chance to find their nature object. Then return to your classroom, and let kids mount the items on the poster board with tape.

Say→ Jasmine saw items she hadn't noticed before. We found wonderful nature items that remind us that God has created a beautiful world. As beautiful as God's creation is, God is even more beautiful.

If you live in an urban area, and the kids have difficulty finding items of nature, you can still have them go outside and look at the sky, sand, and clouds. When you return to the class, simply have the kids share their observations of nature.

Read Psalm 8:1 aloud.

Say→ When we look at the nature God created, it helps us to remember how great God is because nature reflects God's glory.

Ask→ • What things can we see in nature that remind us of God?

• Why should we worship God and not his creation?

• What is your favorite thing in nature that helps you to remember God?

LONELINESS

Scripture: Psalm 25:16

Movie Title:
MUPPETS FROM SPACE (G)

You can also use this clip to discuss the importance of family.

Start Time: 9 minutes

Where to Begin: Lightning flashes in the clouds.

Where to End: Rizzo says, "Maybe it's the rat who's hanging out of the window!"

Plot: All the other Muppets seem to belong to a family or group, and Gonzo feels lonely and left out. He's not like any other creature and begins to believe he might be from outer space.

Review: When Gonzo feels lonely, he finds comfort in the far-out possibility that he might be an alien. Use this clip to show kids that when they feel lonely they can simply turn to God.

NOW PLAYING

Have children form pairs, and have partners each link arms at their elbows and place their free hands on their own hips to create a possible link for another partner. Ideally you'll have one child left who can be the "Tagger" in this Tag game. If not, choose two children to be Taggers at the same time.

Say→ The person who is the Tagger will be chasing the people linked at the elbows. Instead of tagging you, the Tagger will try to link up with your free arm that's on your hip. If the Tagger links up with you, then your original partner must unlink arms with you, and that person becomes the new Tagger. Then you keep on playing!

After playing for several minutes, gather children and

Ask→ • Which did you like better, being without a partner and being the Tagger or being linked to a partner? Why?

• When do you like being alone?

• When do you like being hooked up with a friend?

Say→ I'm going to show you a clip from *Muppets From Space*. Notice how Gonzo feels about being alone.

Show the clip.

Ask→ • How did Gonzo feel about being alone?

• Have you ever felt this way?

• What does it feel like when no one seems to understand you?

• How does it feel to be alone? to be left out?

• How can you tell if someone else is feeling left out or excluded?

• What should you do when you know someone is feeling this way?

Say→ In Psalm 25:16 the writer says, "Turn to me and be gracious to me, for I am lonely and afflicted." This person is talking to God.

Ask→ • How can God help us when we're feeling lonely?

• How can we help others or let God use us to help others not feel lonely?

• What are ways we can turn to others and be gracious to them?

MUSIC

Scripture: Psalm 100:2

 Movie Title:
AN AMERICAN TAIL: FIEVEL GOES WEST (G)

You can also use this clip to discuss getting along with those who are different from you.

Start Time: 49 minutes, 15 seconds

Where to Begin: Tonya Mousekewitz is introduced to the crowd of cats.

Where to End: Tonya concludes her song to cheers from the cats.

Plot: Tonya, a mouse, loves to sing. She gets her big break with an opportunity to sing for a large crowd of cats. The cats are shocked at first to see a mouse, but they are won over by her singing talent.

Review: You can use this scene to teach children about music and the effect it can have on people. Music used as a way to worship God can have a great effect on people, much like Tonya's song influenced the cats. It is a source of encouragement for Christians and a way to open the hearts of all who hear it.

 Supplies: CD player and one or more familiar worship CDs for children

now Playing

Say➜ We're going to watch a scene from *An American Tail: Fievel Goes West*. Fievel's sister, Tonya, loves to sing, and now she gets her big break. The problem is she's a mouse, and she'll be singing for a crowd of cats.

Show the clip.

Ask➜ • How do you feel about the way the cats responded to Tonya's singing?

• What kind of music do you like to listen to?

• How often do you listen to music?

• What kind of feelings can music bring?

Say➜ Psalm 100:2 says, "Worship the Lord with gladness; come before him with joyful songs."

Ask➜ • Why do we sing songs at church?

• How do the songs we sing help us worship God?

• What's your favorite song that we sing at church?

• How does it make you feel to sing praise songs?

Play the beginning of several familiar worship songs that are used in your ministry, and see how quickly kids can guess the name of the song. After several rounds let children choose one of the songs to sing in worship to God.

GOD'S ACCEPTANCE

Scripture: Psalm 100:3

 *Movie Title:*
SHREK (PG)

Start Time: 1 hour, 10 minutes

Where to Begin: Ogre splashes water with her hand.

Where to End: Shrek says, "Yeah, well it does."

Plot: Princess Fiona appears as a beautiful princess by day but turns into an ogre at nightfall. She worries others won't like her when they know what she really is—an ogre. When her true nature is revealed, she's surprised by the reactions of others.

Review: Everyone worries about what others think of them, and many learn to hide behind "masks" so others won't know their true nature. The truth is that God created us and loves us no matter what we look like, no matter who we are. Use this clip to help children understand God loves them and accepts them without any masks or false fronts.

Supplies: Bible, construction paper, scissors, glitter, glue sticks, and markers

now PLAYING

Let each child use the supplies to create a mask that represents how they think other people see them. For example, a child might draw pictures of sporting equipment if others see the child as athletic. When everyone is finished, have kids get in groups of three or four and explain their masks.

Then have everyone gather together and ask:

Ask→ • How's your mask like or unlike the person you are on the inside?

• What people in your life only see your mask?

• What people see you without the mask?

• What makes people afraid to remove their masks and let others see them as they really are?

Say→ Everyone wears a mask from time to time. It's the image we want others to believe is the real us when we're too afraid of what they will think when they know the real us. Watch this movie clip to see how Princess Fiona worries about how Shrek will react if he were to discover who she really is.

Show the *Shrek* clip.

Ask→ • Do you think Princess Fiona's fears are reasonable? Why or why not?

• What surprised you about Shrek's reaction?

• When was a time you felt someone unfairly judged you before knowing all the facts?

Read aloud Psalm 100:3.

Say→ No matter where we go or what kind of mask we put on, God knows everything about us. He knew each of us, even before we were born. And God, who knows us fully, loves us and accepts us unconditionally.

Ask→ • What can you do to accept people for who they are?

• What masks do you need to remove?

• Name one inner quality you can celebrate about yourself this week.

Close in prayer for the children and the qualities they want to celebrate.

WORSHIP

Scripture: Psalm 150

Movie Title:

THE PRINCESS DIARIES (G)

You can also use this clip to discuss popularity.

Start Time: 1 hour, 6 minutes, 42 seconds

Where to Begin: A limousine with flags is pulling up to Mia Thermopolis' school. A reporter says, "Here she is; this is the possible new princess of Genovia right here."

Where to End: Mia goes inside the school.

Plot: This modern fairy tale tells of an awkward fifteen-year-old who learns she's a princess. Suddenly she goes from being an overlooked teen to a cultural idol.

Review: Children can easily identify with the worship of cultural heroes such as movie stars, athletes, and singers. This clip shows that kind of worship and lets you compare it to worshipping God.

Supplies: Paper and pens

now PLAYING

Distribute paper and pens, and have children give each other their autographs. Allow several minutes for kids to exchange their signatures, then gather kids together.

Ask→ • Are these autographs valuable to you? Why or why not?

• What kind of autographs would be valuable to you and why?

Say→ We like to get a little piece of famous people to let others know we've been near them. We also like to praise famous people. What are ways we do that?

This clip from *The Princess Diaries* can help us see how people might praise or even worship famous people. Mia is a regular fifteen-year-old who learns she's really a princess. Watch the reaction of her friends and classmates!

Show *The Princess Diaries* clip.

Ask→ • What did you see happening with her friends?

• In what ways were they worshipping her or praising her?

• Who are other people that we might be tempted to worship?

Say→ Psalm 150 tells us about worshipping God.

Read Psalm 150 aloud.

Ask→ • Why is it so important to praise and worship God?

• How should we praise God?

- **What are reasons to worship God?**

- **Why is it hard for people to worship God, but it's easy to worship a rock star, or an athlete, or a princess?**

Say→ It may be easier to worship people because we can see them, but the Bible makes it clear that we are only to worship God. And God left *his* autograph by giving us his words, the Bible. One way we can worship God is by treasuring God's word in our lives.

PARENTS

Scripture: Proverbs 1:8-9

Movie Title:
A CHRISTMAS STORY (PG)

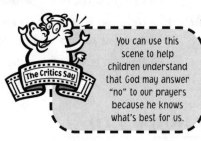

The Critics Say

You can use this scene to help children understand that God may answer "no" to our prayers because he knows what's best for us.

Start Time: 6 minutes, 25 seconds

Where to Begin: The family is eating breakfast, and Ralphie thinks, "Meanwhile, I struggled for the right BB gun hint."

Where to End: After Ralphie tells his mother he wants a Red Ryder BB gun for Christmas, she says, "BB guns are dangerous. I don't want anybody shooting his eye out."

Plot: Ralphie really wants a Red Ryder BB gun for Christmas and is trying to find a way to tell his mother. When he finally does, all she can say is, "You'll shoot your eye out."

Review: Use this lesson to help children understand their parents love them and want what's best for them. Sometimes the decisions their parents make are for their own good and might not be what they want. Sometimes parents have to tell their children no because what they want may be harmful to them.

The water game should be played outside.

The Critics Say

Supplies: Water balloons

Preshow: Fill the balloons with water.

NOW PLAYING

Have children form pairs, and give each pair a water balloon. Tell pairs they are now the proud parents of a water balloon. Have pairs line up so they are facing each other and then gently toss the balloon back and forth. Each time the balloon is caught, both partners should take a step backwards. Children should continue tossing and stepping back until their balloon breaks. See which pair can move the farthest apart before their balloon breaks. Then go inside.

Ask→ • **Do you think you did a good job taking care of your balloon baby? Why or why not?**

- **How could you have been better balloon parents?**

Say→ Let's watch a scene from a movie to see how a mother tries to take care of her son.

Show the clip from *A Christmas Story*.

Say→ Parents want the best for their children. Sometimes the things we want aren't what's best for us so our parents have to say no. The Bible tells us we are to listen to our parents—that we will be blessed if we do.

Ask→
- **Have you ever asked for something you really wanted or wanted to do, and your parents told you no?**
- **How did you feel when they told you no?**
- **How do you know your parents want what's best for you?**

CHOICES (1)

Scripture: Proverbs 1:10-19

 Movie Title:
JUNGLE BOOK 2 (G)

You can also use this clip to teach children about disobedience or peer pressure.

Start Time: 11 minutes, 25 seconds

Where to Begin: Shanti yells "Stop!" as Mowgli leads kids across the river.

Where to End: Mowgli looks out his window toward the jungle and says, "Oh Baloo."

Plot: Mowgli has been told to stay out of the dangerous jungle, but he ignores his family's rules by beginning to cross the river. He is caught, and his new father reveals his disappointment in Mowgli's disobedience. Mowgli, feeling rejected by his new family, considers running away.

Review: The verses in Proverbs discuss how important it is to choose the right path instead of heading down the path of dishonesty. God's disappointment in his people's poor choices is reflected in *Jungle Book 2*—Mowgli's new father is disappointed in Mowgli's disobedience. The clip ends with Mowgli pondering the decision to run away; this point of decision is a great teaching moment for asking about what the right, honest choices are to make in his situation.

Supplies: Bible, masking tape, scissors, and orange and yellow construction paper

Preshow: Place two masking tape lines on the floor, about fifteen feet long and about ten feet apart. Cut out ten to fifteen oval shapes from the orange paper for "mangoes," and about ten to fifteen banana shapes from the yellow paper for "bananas."

now PLAYING

Have the children stand behind one of the masking tape lines. Behind the other masking tape line, scatter the mangoes and bananas. Choose one person to be the Tiger, and have that person stand on the same side as the mangoes and bananas.

Say➜ **Let's play a game called Don't Cross the River. When I say go, you're going to try and get across the river, grab a mango or banana, and get back across the river safely without getting tagged by the Tiger. If you get tagged, you become a Tiger too. You can only grab one piece of fruit at a time.**

Begin the game, and play until everyone becomes a Tiger. After you've played one round, gather the children together.

Say➜ **Knowing whether you should cross the river was an important choice in this game. Let's watch what happens to a little boy, Mowgli, when he has to make this decision.**

Show the *Jungle Book 2* clip.

Ask➜ • **Why was Mowgli's father so disappointed in him?**

• **Do you think Mowgli will go back across the river?**

• **What are some things your parents might tell you to do that you don't want to do?**

Read aloud Proverbs 1:10-19.

Say➜ **There are many times when we might want to "cross the river" and do something we shouldn't. This verse talks about a situation you may never be in. If someone asked you to kill an innocent person, you could probably say no pretty easily. And if they even told you that killing this person would make you really rich, you'd probably still say no. But there might be a different situation you're in where someone wants you to disobey God, like not being honest with your parents or being mean to someone. And just like this proverb says, going along with people who do the wrong thing can make things worse. Be sure to ask God for help when you need to know the right thing to do.**

CHOICES (2)

Scripture: Proverbs 2:6-8

 Movie Title:
JIMMY nEUTROn: BOY GENIUS (PG)

You can also use this clip to teach children about obeying parents.

Start Time: 24 minutes, 45 seconds

Where to Begin: Jimmy and his dad are in Jimmy's room. Jimmy says, "But Dad, all my friends are going to be there."

Where to End: Jimmy says, "We're sneaking out!"

Plot: Jimmy wants to go to the grand opening of an amusement park on a school night. His parents tell him no. He weighs his options and decides that he will sneak out.

Review: You can use this scene to talk about bad choices and how they have consequences. Jimmy has to decide to do what is right or go against the answer his parents gave him. We're all faced with decisions related to good or bad choices. We can choose to follow God's will or do what we want.

 Supplies: Coins

NOW PLAYING

Give each student a coin.

Say→ We're going to flip our coins at the same time. We'll flip them several times. Before each flip you must choose which side of the coin you think will land facing up, either "heads" or "tails." Keep track of how many times you guess right and how many times you guess wrong.

Have the children flip the coins several times.

Ask→ • Did anyone choose right every time?

• How many times did you choose correctly?

• How many times did you choose wrong?

• How is choosing "heads" or "tails" in this game different from choosing between right and wrong in life?

Collect the coins.

Say→ We're going to watch a scene from *Jimmy Neutron: Boy Genius*. Jimmy wants to go to the grand opening of a new amusement park. His parent's tell him no. Let's see what he decides to do.

Show the *Jimmy Neutron: Boy Genius* clip.

Ask→ • What were Jimmy's options?

• How do you feel about the choice he made?

• When you're in situations like this, how do you know how to make the right choice?

Have a volunteer read Proverbs 2:6-8 aloud.

Ask→ • How does this verse give us guidance in making good choices?

• What does the Bible say God will do if we follow him?

PUNISHMENT

Scripture: Proverbs 2:11-12

Movie Title:
A CHRISTMAS STORY (G)

This clip is great for teaching about lying or blaming others.

The Critics Say

Start Time: 41 minutes, 55 seconds

Where to Begin: Ralphie has soap in his mouth for saying a bad word.

Where to End: Ralphie is crying in bed and thinks, "Three blocks away, Schwartz was getting his."

Plot: Ralphie has just said a bad word, and he gets his mouth washed out with soap. Ralphie deceitfully blames a friend, and he listens while his friend is disciplined for something he didn't do. Ralphie ends up crying in bed.

Review: Ralphie knows if he tells the truth in his situation, he will be punished. He thinks telling a lie will help him, but it only results in his friend being disciplined as well. This segment is great for teaching how to face discipline when you do wrong, to admit your mistakes, and accept the consequences.

Supplies: Contact paper, construction paper, scissors, dish soap, and crayons or markers

Preshow: Before class, cut out a 2-inch circle of contact paper for each child.

NOW PLAYING

Ask→ • What kinds of punishment will your parents give you if you say a bad word?

Say→ We're going to watch a part of the movie, *A Christmas Story*. Ralphie has just said a bad word. Let's watch.

Show the *Christmas Story* clip.

Ask→ • Do you think eating soap will help Ralphie keep from swearing?

• Why do you think he got his friend in trouble, too?

• Why do you think Ralphie was crying and upset with his mom?

Hand out construction paper, contact paper circles, scissors, and markers.

Say→ Sometimes, when we do things that are wrong, we try to cover up by doing something else wrong. It can be hard to accept punishment, and we get mad at who's punishing us. But it's better to ask God for forgiveness and realize that our punishment helps us. Fold your paper in half, and draw a circle in the middle on the front. Cut out that circle, then draw Ralphie on the front, using the circle as his mouth.

When kids are done, go around with the dish soap, and have kids open their cards. Add a drop or two of dish soap to the inside of the card, then have kids cover up the soap with the contact paper.

Say→ **On the front of your card, write some things you've done wrong before. It might be fighting, lying, teasing, or disobeying. Then open your card. Ask God what he would want you to do after you've done something wrong.**

Have kids sit quietly and talk to God, asking him how they can get right with God again after they've done something wrong.

Say→ **On the inside of the card, write something positive God would want to happen to you because of your punishment. You might write help others, know what's right, or love each other. Next time you're sent to your room for discipline, read your card. Ask God to help you with anger and sadness while you're punished, then ask him to help you learn from your mistakes.**

PRIDE

Scripture: Proverbs 11:2

You can also use this clip to teach children about perseverance and teamwork.

Movie Title:
SNOW DOGS (PG)

Start Time: 41 minutes

Where to Begin: Ted flips through a manual and reads, "Place your feet on runners."

Where to End: Ted screams, "Bad dogs! Bad dogs!" as he's being dragged by the sled dogs.

Plot: Ted has inherited a dog sled team. He is determined to prove he can get the dogs under his control. He has plenty of trouble trying to do this all on his own.

Review: You can use this scene to teach children about the problems with pride. Ted learns that pride and stubbornness can get you into trouble. The Bible also warns us about having pride in ourselves. We are called to put our trust in God and to rely on Him for all of our needs.

 Supplies: Paper and markers

NOW PLAYING

Give each student a piece of paper, and set the markers out for the group.

Say→ **I want you to make an award for yourself based on several things you do well. You may write out things you are good at, and you may draw pictures as well. Spend a few minutes designing yourself a nice award for the things you are good at.**

Allow students several minutes to design their awards. Encourage creativity in their designs.

Ask→ • **How did it make you feel as you created your own award?**

• **How would you feel showing your award to someone who can do these things better than you?**

Say→ We're going to watch a scene from *Snow Dogs*. Ted has just inherited a team of sled dogs. He is determined to learn how to control them by himself. Let's watch and see how successful he is.

Show the *Snow Dogs* clip.

Ask→ • **What could Ted have done differently?**

• **How would getting help from someone else have made his task easier?**

Say→ Proverbs 11:2 says, "When pride comes, then comes disgrace, but with humility comes wisdom."

Ask→ • **What are some problems pride can cause us?**

• **What does humility look like?**

• **How do you feel about asking others for help?**

Give each child a new piece of paper, and have kids make awards for someone who has been helpful to them.

GRADES

Scripture: Proverbs 14:23

You can also use this clip to teach children about hard work.

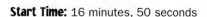

Movie Title:
LITTLE DOGS ON THE PRAIRIE: LYIN', CHEATIN' AND A HOT LOLLIPOP (NOT RATED)

Start Time: 16 minutes, 50 seconds

Where to Begin: Hollister says, "What's with all this cheatin'? I don't remember these tests being this hard."

Where to End: Darcy answers, "Just you!"

Plot: Test grades are under suspicion as the little prairie dogs are getting the same spelling words wrong. While talking to the teacher and trying to figure out if cheating is going on, the older prairie dogs are forced to make up a difficult test they had skipped many years before.

Review: You can use this scene to lead children in a discussion about grades. The prairie dogs are suspected of cheating on hard tests in order to get a better grade. The older prairie dogs had even skipped tests because they were so difficult. The results we see from our work, and the grades we get, are a reflection of the effort we have put into that work.

 Supplies: Several small, easy puzzles and a watch with a second hand

NOW PLAYING

Have students get into groups of three or four. Give each group the pieces to a puzzle. Have them work together as a group to put their puzzle together as you time them. Announce the times for each team. Have groups switch puzzles and try to beat their previous time. You may stop after a few rounds or when every group has had a turn to complete each puzzle.

Ask→ • Did trying to beat the other groups affect how difficult is was to put your puzzle together?

• How did you feel while working on the puzzles?

Say→ We're going to watch a scene from *Little Dogs on the Prairie: Lyin', Cheatin' and a Hot Lollipop.* Here the prairie dogs are faced with difficult spelling tests. The pressure has caused some to skip tests and some to be suspected of cheating.

Show the clip.

Ask→ • How important are grades to you?

• How do you feel when you have a difficult test to take?

Say→ Proverbs 14:23 says, "All hard work brings a profit, but mere talk leads only to poverty."

Ask→ • What are the benefits of hard work in school?

• Where else, besides school, can hard work be a benefit?

• What will help you work hard in school?

ANGER

Scripture: Proverbs 15:1

 Movie Title:
THE LITTLE RASCALS (1994) (PG)

You can also use this clip to teach about placing blame on others.

Start Time: 54 minutes

Where to Begin: Alfalfa's talent act has just failed, and he and Spanky begin to argue over whose fault all the mishaps are.

Where to End: Alfalfa says, "I'd quit!" and storms off from the group of boys.

Plot: Spanky and Alfalfa get into a name-calling match as they argue over who's gotten them into all their troubles.

Review: Use this scene to demonstrate that anger, calling names, and shouting don't solve anything. Letting our anger take over and saying things we really don't mean does more harm than good. People are more willing to listen to us if we speak to them in a controlled, respectful manner.

now PLAYING

Say→ We're going to watch a scene from *The Little Rascals*. Spanky and Alfalfa are angry with each other and say a lot of things they probably don't mean.

Show the clip.

Have children form pairs.

Say→ Think of a time when you were really angry with someone. Share with your partner how you reacted.

Be sure to emphasize the way Spanky and Alfalfa were acting is *not* the way God would have us react. name-calling is never an acceptable response when we're angry.

Allow a few minutes for the children to share.

Have someone read Proverbs 15:1 out loud.

Say→ The Bible tells us that when we're angry with someone, we should still be kind in the things we say. Share with your partner how you could have reacted differently when you were angry.

After several minutes of discussion, let several pairs share their examples.

Ask→ • How do you feel when someone is angry with you and calls you a name?

• What are ways to handle yourself when you're angry that don't include shouting or calling names?

Say→ Sometimes it's not easy to control our temper. It's in those times we need to pray and call on God to calm us down and show us how to react. We need to think about what we say before we say it. Being angry isn't wrong, but what we *do* with that anger can get us in trouble.

FRIENDS

Scripture: Proverbs 17:17

Movie Title:
SPACE JAM (G)

You can also use this clip to teach children about sacrifice.

Start Time: 1 hour, 2 minutes, 45 seconds

Where to Begin: During a timeout in the game, Michael Jordan says, "Hey!" An alien replies, "Are you talking to me?"

Where to End: Michael says, "Deal" as he and the alien shake on their agreement.

Plot: The aliens have taken the talent away from five professional basketball players. Michael Jordan makes a deal with the aliens to get their talent back if Michael's team wins. If the aliens win, they will get to keep Michael for their circus.

Review: You can use this scene to teach children about true friends. Michael was willing to put himself at risk to help his friends. That's the kind of friend Jesus is to us, and that's the kind of friend we can become for others.

Supplies: Individually wrapped candies

Allergy **ALERT**

NOW PLAYING

Give each child a piece of candy, and ask kids to not open or eat the candy yet.

Say→ I'm sure most of you like candy a lot and are glad to have a piece. But are any of you willing to give up your candy for someone else? If so give your candy to someone else right now.

Stress that this is entirely voluntary—no one is required to give up his or her candy. Have children make their decisions.

Ask→ • Was this a hard or easy decision to make? Why?

• What are things you would be willing to give up for a friend?

• What are things you would not be willing to give up?

Say→ We're going to watch a scene from *Space Jam*. Here Michael Jordan makes a deal to help five of his professional basketball friends who have had their talent taken away by aliens. Let's watch to see what Michael is willing to risk for his friends.

Show the *Space Jam* clip.

Ask→ • What did you see in this clip that you would like to find in a friend?

Say→ Proverbs 17:17 says, "A friend loves at all times."

Ask→ • How can friends show love?

• How can having good friends help us in our lives?

• What important things will you look for in a friend?

BULLIES

Scripture: Proverbs 19:19

Movie Title:
MONSTERS, INC. (G)

You can also use this clip to teach children about friendship.

Start Time: 10 minutes, 39 seconds

Where to Begin: In the locker room, Mike says, "You know pal, she's the one."

Where to End: Mike says, "One of these days I'm really going to let you teach that guy a lesson!"

Plot: Sulley is close to setting the all-time scare record for Monsters, Inc., but Randall is close behind. Randall sneaks into the locker room, scares Mike, and bullies him. Mike talks back, but relies on his larger friend Sulley to back him up.

Review: You can use this scene to show students that it's not good to bully other people or put them down. Randall intimidated Mike making him feel afraid and uneasy. It was more than mere teasing based on the way it made Mike feel in the situation.

> If a child shares that he or she is being bullied, be sure to offer support and talk to the parents. Do what you can to protect your children.

The Critics Say

 Supplies: Building blocks

NOW PLAYING

Help children form two groups, and give them the blocks. Assign one group as the "builders" and one the "bullies."

Say→ The builders must try to stack blocks to get as many tall buildings as they can. The bullies will be allowed to take one block at a time and put it back into the pile. Bullies can take one block as often as they like. Begin!

Stop the game before it gets hopelessly frustrating. Have teams switch their roles and play again. Stop the game again after a few minutes, and put the blocks away.

Ask→ • What was fun or not fun about this game?

• When do you have these feelings of frustration in real life?

Say→ We're going to watch a scene from *Monsters, Inc.* Mike and Sulley are in the locker room when Randall sneaks in and begins picking on Mike. Let's see what happens.

Show the clip.

Ask→ • How do you think Mike felt?

• Have you ever felt like you were being bullied or picked on?

Say→ Proverbs 16:19 says, "Better to be lowly in spirit and among the oppressed than to share plunder with the proud."

Ask→ • What do you think this means?

• How would it make others feel if you bullied them?

Say→ It's not fun for us to be bullied. Since we know what that feels like, we need to be careful not to bully other people.

BRAGGING (1)

Scripture: Proverbs 27:1

Movie Title:
ICE AGE (PG)

You can also use this clip to teach children about friendship and facing difficult situations.

Start Time: 12 minutes, 7 seconds

Where to Begin: Manny is carrying a huge load of wood while Sid drags only half a stick.

Where to End: Sid takes shelter under Manny's tail.

Plot: Sid and Manny end up together as cold weather approaches. Sid brags about the fire he is going to start and the ease in which he will do it. After much time and effort, and a good bit of rain also, Sid finally gives up and has to eat his words.

Review: You can use this scene to help children see that bragging can be dangerous since we cannot control things as much as we would like. Sid had to accept the fact that he was not going to be able to build the fire he had promised. He could not control the weather. We can learn that we should trust in God instead of our own efforts.

Supplies: Masking tape, hardcover book, and several building blocks or other stackable objects

Preshow: Create a course setting up a start and finish line by placing masking tape on the floor. Have several building blocks and a hardcover book at the start line ready for students to carry across the finish line.

NOW PLAYING

Show students the course with start and finish lines. Show them the blocks, and let them know they will be challenged to carry a stack of blocks

If you have more than ten children in your group, set up two or more obstacle courses.

on the hardcover book all the way through the course. Have students line up behind the start line.

Say→ **Everyone will get a chance to carry a stack of blocks on top of this book and walk through the course. When it's your turn, hold the book, and tell me how many blocks you think you can carry in your stack without dropping them.**

Allow each child a turn at carrying the blocks through the course.

Ask→ • **Who thinks they can carry the most blocks through the course walking backwards and carrying the book with just one hand?**

• **How many can you carry?**

Have the child who thinks he or she can carry the most blocks in this way try to complete the course. Cheer the child on, and then finish with a round of applause for all.

Say→ We're going to watch a scene from *Ice Age*. Sid is bragging to Manny about how he's going to build a fire, but the weather doesn't cooperate. Let's see how well he does.

Show the *Ice Age* clip.

Ask→ • How would you have felt if you were Sid?

Say→ Proverbs 27:1 says, "Do not boast about tomorrow, for you do not know what a day may bring forth."

Ask→ • How can bragging be dangerous?

• Why should we avoid bragging?

• How do you feel when someone else brags?

Say→ One way to avoid bragging is to brag about someone else!

BRAGGING (2)

Scripture: Proverbs 27:2

 Movie Title:
THE IRON GIANT (PG)

Start Time: 48 minutes

Where to Begin: Hogarth climbs on a rock and calls, "Hey, Dean! Watch this!"

Where to End: A pig farmer talks to the drenched Dean and drives away. Dean says, "I think that's enough fun for one day."

Plot: Hogarth and his adult friend, Dean, have befriended a giant robot. Because the government wants to destroy the robot, they have to keep their friend a secret, but because of his gigantic size, this isn't easy.

Review: When Hogarth, Dean, and the robot head to the local swimming hole, Hogarth decides to show off a little. His words and actions are silly, especially when they're compared to the actions of the robot. This fun clip reminds kids that instead of bragging and showing off, we should use our words and actions to praise others.

Supplies: Bible, paper, and pen

Preshow: Prepare slips of paper with different things kids can brag about, such as "My mom is smarter than your mom," "I can do more tricks on my skateboard than you," or "My grades are the highest in my school."

now PLAYING

Say→ We all know someone who likes to brag or show off. Let's have some fun by having a contest to see who's the best at bragging and showing off!

Form pairs. Have each pair draw a slip of paper and brag about what's on its slip. Encourage kids to ham it up. After each pair has had a turn, applaud for everyone without declaring anyone a winner.

Say→ There's a funny scene from the movie *The Iron Giant* that involves a little bragging and showing off. Let's watch.

Show the clip.

Ask→ • **What were the consequences of Hogarth's bragging and showing off?**

• **Have you ever had an experience where bragging or showing off had bad consequences? If so, what happened?**

• **How do you feel when someone else is showing off or bragging? Explain.**

• **Is bragging and showing off wrong? Why or why not?**

Read Proverbs 27:2.

Ask→ • **What does this verse say about bragging and showing off?**

• **How can this verse help us the next time we feel like bragging about ourselves?**

Say→ Let's practice praising one another just as Proverbs 27:2 says.

Close by having partners affirm each other with a sincere word of praise.

POVERTY

Scripture: Matthew 6:19-21

 Movie Title:
IT'S A WONDERFUL LIFE (NOT RATED)

The Critics Say

You can use this clip to teach the value of friendship and also the concept of sowing and reaping.

Start Time: 2 hours, 4 minutes, 41 seconds

Where to Begin: Mary leads George and the children into the living room.

Where to End: Harry toasts George as "the richest man in town."

Plot: George has just returned from a fanciful journey to see what Bedford Falls would be like if he had never lived. Meanwhile Mary had spread the word about their financial crisis. The whole town of Bedford Falls shows up to contribute what they can to keep George from bankruptcy.

Review: Jesus has told us to "store up treasure in heaven." Practically speaking, this means putting others' needs before our own desires and comforts. Throughout *It's a Wonderful Life*, George Bailey does exactly that. Though he dreams of traveling the world, he sacrificially gives up his own opportunities to help others. In the end, George is rewarded when all the lives *he* has touched—his "treasures"—come back to rescue him.

 Supplies: Bible, paper, and pencils

now PLAYING

Say→ We're going on a treasure hunt. But this time the "hunt" takes place in your heart!

Arrange the kids in groups of four. Distribute paper and pencils to each group. Make sure each group appoints a recorder to take notes for the group.

Say→ I'm going to give your group two minutes to brainstorm all the things you "treasure." Aim for the most original answers you can think of. Any questions?

When the two minutes are up, have one person from each group read their answers.

Ask→ • What were some of the similarities in our lists?

• What do these similarities tell us about the kinds of things we value?

• What answers surprised you?

Say→ Jesus was pretty clear in explaining what we should treasure.

Read Matthew 6:19-21.

Say→ If we store up treasure in heaven, then we're *not* valuing material things. We value the kinds of things that last forever, like our relationship with God and our friendships with others. These are things money can't buy.

Let's watch a clip from *It's a Wonderful Life*. Before this scene of the movie, George's family business was headed for bankruptcy because of an error made by his elderly uncle. George thinks about taking his own life, until he's visited by an angel who shows him how different—and how sad—the town would be if he had never lived. In this scene George has recently "come back to life."

Show the movie clip.

Ask→ • Why do you think all the townspeople showed up to help George?

• What did Harry really mean when he said that George was "the richest man in town"?

• How can we get this same kind of "wealth"?

GOD'S LOVE

Scripture: Romans 8:37-39

Movie Title:
JACK FROST (1998) (PG)

> **The Critics Say**
> Remind children that this story is just pretend, and that only God can bring life after death.

Start Time: 1 hour 29 minutes, 56 seconds

Where to Begin: Charlie wakes up and says, "It's Christmas!"

Where to End: When Jack Frost, the snowman, says, "If you ever need me, I'll be right here. You just call me."

Plot: Jack Frost is a dad whose life is cut short by a car accident. A year after his death he visits his family as a snowman.

Review: While death does separate Charlie from his father, this movie shows that a father's love is always with his son. In a much greater way, literally nothing can separate us from the love of our heavenly Father.

now PLAYING

Have children stand in a circle, shoulder to shoulder. Tell them to try to keep you from separating them. Then use every move possible to get between the kids. Squeeze between tiny gaps, crawl between spaces near the floor, try to distract the kids then get through, and so on. If you do get through the circle, let a child take your place, and play again as time allows.

Ask➜ • What could have made it impossible for me to separate you from each other?

• What are things we don't want to be separated from?

Say➜ None of us want to be separated from our parents. Let's watch this scene from *Jack Frost*. Charlie's dad has died. But through a twist of movie magic, his dad comes back as a snowman! In this scene Jack is saying goodbye to his son. Watch this.

Show the *Jack Frost* clip.

Ask➜ • Why did Jack point to Charlie's heart?

• How do you think that made Charlie feel to know he was going to be separated from his dad?

Say➜ God is our heavenly Father, and we don't want to be separated from him either. Let's read what the Bible has to say about this.

Have children read Romans 8:37-39 in their Bibles.

Ask➜ • Can anything separate us from God's love? Why or why not?

• How do you feel about this?

Say➜ It's great to know there is a Father who will never, ever leave us!

FITTING IN

Scripture: Romans 15:7

Movie Title:
OLIVER & COMPANY (G)

You can also use this clip to teach children about friendship and bullying.

The Critics Say

Start Time: 21 minutes, 50 seconds

Where to Begin: Desoto says, "Hey Roscoe, look what I found."

Where to End: Fagin says, "We've never had a cat in the gang before. We can use all the help we can get."

Plot: Oliver, who was all alone in New York City, hooks up with Dodger to get some food and ends up following him to his hideout. Oliver gets backed into a corner when Desoto and Roscoe show up to pick on Dodger's ragged gang of dogs. After clawing back at the larger dogs, Oliver is accepted into the gang in spite of being a cat.

Review: You can use this scene to teach children about fitting in and accepting others. The gang accepting Oliver is a good picture of what the church should be like. We can all do our part in showing God's love by overcoming the differences we have and looking at each other as God does.

NOW PLAYING

Say→ We're going to watch a scene from *Oliver & Company*. Oliver follows Dodger back to the dog's hideout. Let's watch and see how well this cat fits in with the gang of dogs.

Show the *Oliver & Company* clip.

Ask→ • How do you think Oliver felt before he was accepted into the gang?

• How do you think Oliver felt after he was accepted into the gang?

Say→ We're going to play a game now. I need everyone to get into two lines facing each other. You'll need to be facing a partner in the other line.

After students are in two even lines facing each other, choose one line to be the "mirror" line. Students in this line will try to be like a mirror imitating everything their partners do. After a minute or so, switch and let the other line be the mirrors. You may also have them switch partners if you would like to do several short rounds.

Ask→ • How hard was it to be just like your partner?

• Have you ever wanted to be like someone else to feel like you fit in? If so, what happened?

Say→ Romans 15:7 says, "Accept one another, then, just as Christ accepted you, in order to bring praise to God."

Ask→ • **How do you feel when you are around people you don't know very well?**

• **How do you think others feel around you?**

• **What can we do to help others feel accepted and like they fit in at church?**

COMPETITION

Scripture: 1 Corinthians 9:24-25

Movie Title:
AIR BUD: GOLDEN RECEIVER (G)

You can also use this clip to teach children about perseverance and encouragement.

Start Time: 36 minutes, 45 seconds

Where to Begin: Josh says, "...ready, down, set, hut, hike" as he takes over as quarterback and then gets hit hard.

Where to End: Coach says, "It's like you're playing for all the wrong reasons. Football's all about having fun. That's got to be your bottom line, Josh."

Plot: Josh is new to the football team, and now that the first string quarterback is hurt, he gets his chance to play. He lets the pressure get to him and struggles to play at the level he is capable of. Buddy, the dog, gets into the action and helps the team score.

Review: You can use this scene to teach children about the good and bad points of competition. Josh learns that competition can get the best of us when the pressure gets too tough. Competition can be fun as long as we don't take winning or losing too seriously.

Supplies: Two buckets, masking tape, and newspaper

Preshow: Place the buckets on a table with a couple of feet of space between them. Place two masking tape lines on the floor several feet away from the table. Make six newspaper balls by wadding newspaper and wrapping it in tape.

NOW PLAYING

Have children form two teams and line up behind the masking tape lines to shoot free throws.

Say→ **Each person will get three balls to throw, and your team gets one point for each one that lands in your team's bowl.**

Allow each person a turn, and encourage teams to cheer each other on. Keep score and shout the score out frequently.

Say→ **Now we'll award your points to the other team.**

Be ready for a mixture of complaining and cheering. Play again, not telling children if they'll keep their points or give them to the other team after this round. At the end of this round, combine *all* the scores from both rounds, announce the grand total, and congratulate *everyone* for their combined efforts.

Ask→ • How did you feel when the scores were switched in round one?

   • How did you feel when all of the scores were added together at the end?

Say→ We're going to watch a scene from *Air Bud: Golden Receiver.*

   Show the clip.

Ask→ • When can doing our best be good?

   • What if doing our best isn't good enough? How do you feel?

   • How can competition get out of hand?

   Have children read 1 Corinthians 9:24-25 in their Bibles.

Ask→ • What does this verse mean?

   • What is the only prize that's really important in life?

Say→ Playing games and coming out with more or less points is a temporary thing. Following God's will is what is really important, and it's what has a lasting reward.

COURAGE

Scripture: 1 Corinthians 16:13

Movie Title:
THE SANDLOT (PG)

You can also use this clip to teach children about friendship.

Start Time: 1 hour, 18 minutes, 30 seconds

Where to Begin: Scotty says, "Benny wait! It's OK. It was my fault."

Where to End: Benny gets safely back over the fence with the ball. *Note: Be sure to stop immediately at this point as a bad word follows.*

Plot: Scotty has taken a baseball, signed by Babe Ruth, from his stepfather without asking, and it's lost over a fence. The enemy, a very large dog, lives on the other side of the fence. Scotty and his friends have tried unsuccessfully to get the ball back. Now Benny is going to risk jumping the fence to grab the ball away from the dog.

Review: You can use this scene to help children understand true courage. Benny displays courage when he is willing to put his own safety on the line to help get his friend out of trouble. Living for God requires a similar kind of courage.

Supplies: Paper, scissors, glue sticks, and magazines with current event articles

NOW PLAYING

Say→ We're going to watch a scene from *The Sandlot*. Scotty has lost his step-dad's baseball with Babe Ruth's signature on it. His friends are trying to help him get it back while danger waits on the other side of the fence. Benny decides he will face the danger head-on. Let's watch.

Show *The Sandlot* clip.

Ask→ • How would you feel if you were the one getting the baseball?

• If Benny was scared, how was he able to get the ball?

Say→ First Corinthians 16:13 says, "Be on your guard; stand firm in the faith; be men of courage; be strong."

Ask→ • In what way do we need courage to live for God?

• How can we live courageously for God?

Give each student a piece of paper and set the magazines and other supplies out for them to use.

Say→ You are going to make a "courage collage" on your paper by cutting out pictures and words from these magazines. Choose as many items as you can find which make you think of courage.

Allow students plenty of time to find pictures and words that represent courage, cut them out, and glue them to their papers. Then let children share about what they've created and how it will remind them to be courageous.

IMITATING GOD

Scripture: Ephesians 5:1-2

 Movie Title:
101 DALMATIANS (1961) (G)

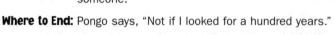

You can also use this clip to discuss judging others by their appearances.

Start Time: 4 minutes

Where to Begin: Pongo, the dog, says, "It was plain to see that my old pet needed someone."

Where to End: Pongo says, "Not if I looked for a hundred years."

Plot: In this scene Pongo is searching for a wife for his master. The dogs and masters he observes all resemble each other. Pongo searches for a pair that will resemble him and his master.

Review: In this clip it's easy for children to identify which pair will make the best mates for Pongo and Roger—it's the pair that are most like them. In the same way, we hope others will be able to identify us as followers of Christ by our actions and attitudes. Use this clip to help children consider what it means to imitate Christ.

Supplies: Index cards and marker

Preshow: Write one of the following words on each index card: *happy, sad, mad, hurt, bored, afraid, shy, confused, tired, frustrated.*

now Playing

Choose a volunteer to come up and draw one of the index cards from the stack. Have the child silently read the card and then face the class and demonstrate this emotion without any words. After the others have correctly guessed the emotion, let another child choose a new card and play again. Play until all the cards have been used.

Ask➔ • **Was it easy or hard to guess the emotions of someone based on their expressions? Why?**

• **What other emotions could you easily express with your face?**

• **What can people tell about you based on your expressions?**

Say➔ **It's not too hard to know something about someone based on that person's face. In this movie clip, a dog is looking for partners for himself and his master and determines who is best based on what he sees. Let's see how he makes his choice.**

Show the *101 Dalmatians* clip.

Ask➔ • **What kind of dog was Pongo looking for?**

• **What could Pongo tell about the other dogs just by looking at them?**

Say➔ **These pets imitated their masters even to the point of looking like them; Jesus has asked us to imitate him too.**

Read Ephesians 5:1-2.

Ask➔ • **What are some of the different ways you've seen people imitate God?**

• **How can you tell if someone is a follower of God or not?**

• **Can people tell by your actions or expressions that you're a follower of God? Why or why not?**

• **What are attitudes or expressions that would let people know you're a follower of God?**

ENCOURAGEMENT

Scripture: 1 Thessalonians 5:11

Movie Title:
D2: THE MIGHTY DUCKS (PG)

Start Time: 55 minutes

You can also use this clip to teach children about helping others.

Where to Begin: Two teams face each other on the playing court, and the older boy says, "My little brother, Russ, here's been tellin' me that you've been chokin' big time."

Where to End: Older brother watches bus go and says, "Go USA. Go get 'em."

Plot: Team USA is struggling to play hockey well enough to win. They get into a rough street hockey game and learn a thing or two. After the game Team USA gets an encouraging send-off as they go to the big game.

Review: You can use this scene to teach children the importance of encouragement. Team USA was getting down, and they needed someone to help get them up for their next big game. It's easy for people to feel down and be hard on themselves. By offering encouragement we can help each other out and fulfill how God wants us to act toward each other.

 Supplies: Index cards, markers, construction paper, scissors, and glue sticks

now playing

Say→ We're going to watch a scene from *D2: The Mighty Ducks*. Team USA is in a slump, and a local team is helping them play better. Let's see how things go.

Show the clip.

Ask→ • How do you think Team USA felt after this game?

• Do you think it will help them in their next game?

Say→ First Thessalonians 5:11 says, "Therefore encourage one another and build each other up, just as in fact you are doing."

Ask→ • How was the team encouraged in the movie?

• In what ways can we encourage each other?

• How do you feel when someone encourages you?

• How do you feel when you encourage someone else?

Say→ We're going to spend some time creating encouraging notes to give away. I want you to think of someone you would like to encourage, and decorate a note card for that person. Before we start let's take time to pray for God's help in encouraging others.

Pray together and then set out the supplies for making encouragement notes. Encourage the students to be creative in their artwork and to be encouraging in the messages they create.

BOREDOM

Scripture: 2 Thessalonians 3:11-13

Movie Title:
3-2-1 PENGUINS: THE AMAZING CARNIVAL OF COMPLAINING

The Critics Say

> You can also use this clip to teach children about attitude, hard work, and complaining.

Start Time: 1 minute

Where to Begin: Scene fades in with a fish on the wall as Jason is thumb wrestling against himself.

Where to End: Michelle says, "Touchy!"

Plot: Jason is bored being at his grandmother's house for the summer. He'd rather be at space camp with his friend. He is trying to find something to do but is unwilling to help his sister and their grandmother plant seeds in the garden.

Review: You can use this scene to help children understand that boredom can be overcome if we are willing to put aside our own desires. Jason wanted to do only what interested him. God wants us to be active in doing what is good. The benefit is not only completing the work that may need to be done but also the mutual encouragement from joining in with others.

NOW PLAYING

Have children form pairs and stand across from each other so there are two lines facing each other.

Ask→ • What fun activity would you like to do right now?

Say→ Those are good ideas, but we're going to try a special activity that you're sure to like. I want everyone to stand as still as possible and stare at your partner. Don't move and don't stop looking at your partner's eyes. On your mark, get set, go!

Let the activity go for a minute or two. When you start getting complaints about how boring it is, you may want to go just a little bit longer. End the activity and have children sit down.

Ask→ • How did you like our opening activity?

Say→ We're going to watch a scene from *3-2-1 Penguins*. Jason and his sister Michelle are spending the summer with their grandmother, but Jason would rather be at space camp. Let's watch and see how he handles it.

Show the clip.

Ask→ • Have you ever felt the way Jason felt in this clip?

• What do you think Jason could have done to keep from feeling bored?

Have children read 2 Thessalonians 3:11-13 in their Bibles.

Ask→ • How do you feel about not getting to do the things you want to do?

• How do you feel about doing things you don't want to do?

• What would be a good response or action the next time you're feeling bored?

THE BIBLE

Scripture: 2 Timothy 3:16-17

Movie Title:
WHAT ABOUT BOB? (PG)

The Critics Say — You can also use this clip to teach the children that we can be excited to share God's Word with others.

Start Time: 1 hour, 7 minutes

Where to Begin: Bob and Dr. Marvin are being interviewed for television in Dr. Marvin's living room. The host says, "Bob, tell us your impressions of *Baby Steps.*"

Where to End: The interviewer says, "Back to you, Joan."

Plot: Bob thinks Dr. Marvin and his book, *Baby Steps*, has changed his life and is eager to tell everyone about it.

Review: *Baby Steps* changed Bob's life in the movie. You can use this scene to help the children understand how the Bible can be a life-changing book. If we apply what it teaches to our lives, we can live a life pleasing to God. The Bible gives us everything we need to know how to live.

Supplies: Cookbook and ingredients for a cookie recipe

Preshow: Choose a favorite cookie recipe from your cookbook, and bring the unassembled ingredients.

Allergy **ALERT**

NOW PLAYING

Set the ingredients for your cookies out on a table.

Ask→ • What would you think if I offered you a cup of flour to eat?

• Would anyone like a raw egg?

• Is there anything up here you would want to eat by itself?

Say→ Not many of these things are very appealing by themselves. But when we put them together, they can make tasty cookies. And to make a cookie, you need the recipe. The recipe can be found in this book.

Hold up your cookbook.

Say→ We can learn different things from different books.

We're going to watch a scene from *What About Bob?* Let's see what Bob thinks of Dr. Marvin's book.

Show the clip.

Ask→ • What made Bob so excited about the book *Baby Steps*?

  • What book should we be as excited to share with others?

Say→ Just as Bob thought Dr. Marvin's book changed his life, we have a book that we know will change our lives. The Bible contains all the instructions we need to lead the kind of life God wants for us. It is our recipe for life.

The Bible was given to us by God to teach us and train us to do his work. As we read it and learn from it, we become more and more the kind of people who God wants us to be.

Ask→ • Bob was excited to share about he book he'd read. How do you feel about sharing the Bible with other people?

CHURCH

Scripture: Hebrews 10:25

 Movie Title:
THE BEST CHRISTMAS PAGEANT EVER (NOT RATED)

You can also use this clip to teach children about accepting others.

Start Time: 9 minutes, 48 seconds

Where to Begin: Boy stops playing basketball and says, "Hey, you give me back my lunch, Leroy!"

Where to End: Girl says, "Before church was even over, they cleaned out the collection plates, scribbled on the Bibles, and stuck gum all over the pews."

Plot: The Herdman kids, a rather large and intimidating family, hear about all the good things you get when you go to church. The next Sunday they are in church to see what it's all about.

Review: You can use this clip to talk about what church is all about. The reason the Herdmans went to church was to get all the good things, like cookies, that they had been told about. Encourage children to consider the other benefits that come from being involved in a church.

 Supplies: Hula-Hoops

NOW PLAYING

Say→ We're going to watch a scene from *The Best Christmas Pageant Ever*. We'll see kids from the Herdman family learn some things about church and decide to go try it out. Their first visit to church is kind of funny as they are just starting to learn what church is really about. Let's watch.

Show *The Best Christmas Pageant Ever* clip.

Ask→ • Why did the Herdman children go to church?

- **What do you like about going to church?**

Have students form groups of three or four. Each group should gather inside a Hula-Hoop, so adjust the size of the groups based on the size of your Hula-Hoops and the size of your children. When each group is inside a hoop, give directions for how children should move—across the room, walk backward, hop three times, and so on. Then have children remove the hoops.

Ask→
- **How easy or hard was this activity?**

- **How does working together in this activity remind you of the ways people work together in a church?**

- **What can you do to be involved in our church?**

Say→ Going to church is a part of being in God's family. Hebrews 10:25 says, "Let us not give up meeting together, as some are in the habit of doing, but let us encourage one another—and all the more as you see the Day approaching.

Ask→
- **In what ways can we encourage each otgher by going to church?**

DISCIPLINE

Scripture: Hebrews 12:11

Movie Title:
SPY KIDS (PG)

You can also use this clip to teach children about obeying parents, hard work, and getting along with others.

Start Time: 8 minutes, 50 seconds

Where to Begin: Juni says, " Why do we have to do this every morning?"

Where to End: Carmen says, "Butter fingers!" and Juni responds, "We'll see about that."

Plot: Carmen and Juni are doing their morning exercises. They're not excited about doing this extra work that their parents require. As the movie progresses, it is evident their hard work will pay off.

Review: You can use this scene to teach children about the benefits of discipline and how discipline can mean instruction or correction. Carmen and Juni learn that discipline pays off when it helps them in the situations they later face. Biblical discipline pays off for us through instruction and training that lead us to know God's will and through correction that draws us back into God's will.

Supplies: Stopwatch and a variety of sport balls and game supplies such as cones, buckets, and bats

Preshow: Place all of the sports items in the middle of your playing area.

now PLAYING

Say→ We're going to watch a scene from *Spy Kids*. Here Carmen and Juni are doing their exercises as their parents have told them. Let's watch and see what they think about doing this.

Show the *Spy Kids* clip.

Ask→ • How would you feel if you had to do the extra work they had to do?

• Why do you think their parents made them do these exercises?

• Why did they need to be so disciplined in their exercises?

Show children the balls and other sports items you have collected.

Say→ Let's think about being disciplined as we play this game. You have two minutes to play it. On your mark, get set, go!

Children may not start right away since there are no clear directions. Encourage them to "Get in there and have fun." Avoid telling them what to do. Keep track of time, and frequently tell them how much is remaining. At the end of the two minutes, have children sit in a circle and discuss the following questions.

Ask→ • How did you like this game?

• What would have made this game better?

Say→ Playing a game without any rules is kind of like living with no discipline. Discipline helps us know what we should and should not do. And, like getting a foul in basketball helps us to play within the rules, discipline as correction helps us to live as God wants us to live.

Hebrews 12:11 says, "No discipline seems pleasant at the time, but painful. Later on, however, it produces a harvest of righteousness and peace for those who have been trained by it."

Ask→ • How can discipline help us?

• How can not having discipline hurt us?

Allow children to choose a game that uses some of the equipment you've provided. Let kids explain the rules, then play as time allows.

HEROES

Scripture: 1 Peter 2:21 and 1 Corinthians 11:1

 Movie Title:

HERCULES (ANIMATED) (G)

Start Time: 25 minutes, 10 seconds

Where to Begin: Hercules sees Phil and asks, "Can you help us?"

You can also use this clip to teach children about commitment.

The Critics Say

Where to End: Hercules says, "But I'm different than those other guys, Phil. I can go the distance."

Plot: Hercules wants to be a hero, and he's looking for someone to show him how. He's directed to Phil and has to plead his case trying to convince Phil to help.

Review: You can use this scene to help children understand that looking up to heroes means we need to choose those role models very carefully. There's no shortage of individuals in our society who try to achieve hero status, but Jesus is our ultimate hero, and those we look to as role models should be following Jesus as well.

Supplies: White T-shirts and markers

Preshow: Place each shirt along with markers in a location where groups of four to six students can work together to decorate the shirt.

now PLAYING

Have children form groups of four to six, and give each group a shirt.

Say→ **Each group is going to create a costume for a new superhero. Be creative in your design, and be prepared to tell us all about the great qualities of your new superhero!**

> **The Critics Say**
> You may use new shirts or good clean used shirts for this activity. Use large shirts so kids can put them on over their clothes.

Allow time for groups to work on their designs. Give them notice for how much time they have left, and then bring them together. Allow each group to show off their design and tell a little about their new superhero. If you like, one child from each group can model the shirt while the others tell about it.

Say→ **We're going to watch a scene from *Hercules*.**

Show the clip.

Ask→ • **What do you think a hero should be like?**

• **What does it take to be a superhero?**

Say→ **First Peter 2:21 says, "To this you were called, because Christ suffered for you, leaving you an example, that you should follow in his steps."**

Ask→ • **What makes Jesus a superhero?**

• **In what ways can we be like Jesus?**

Say→ **In 1 Corinthians 11:1, Paul says, "Follow my example, as I follow the example of Christ."**

Ask→ • **How do you feel about following someone else's example?**

• **How do you feel about setting an example for others?**

TOPICAL INDEX

MOVIE INDEX

the **1**
thing™

that everyone craves.

that really matters.

that gets undivided attention.

that can transform your life.

that encourages pastors.

that will re-energize you.

that will bring you joy.

that will unite your community.

that brings families closer.

that frees you.

that gives you focus.

that answers the why's.

that means true success.

that eliminates distractions.

that gives you real purpose.

that can transform your church.

Discover how *The 1 Thing* can revolutionize the way you approach ministry. It's engaging. Fun. Even shocking. But most of all, it's about re-thinking what "growing a relationship with Jesus" really means. Pick up Thom & Joani Schultz's inspiring new book today.

More Ideas for Your Children's Ministry

from Group Publishing...

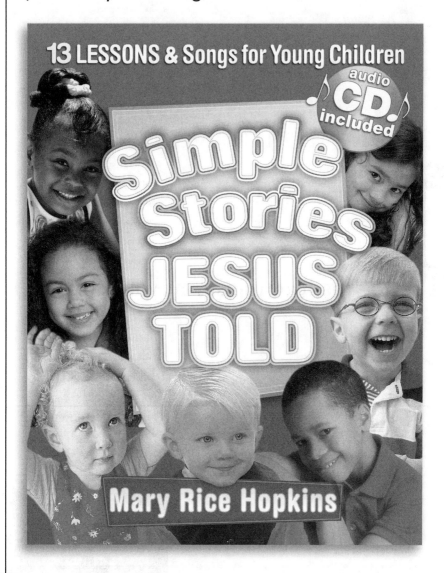

13 LESSONS & Songs for Young Children

audio **CD** *included*

Simple Stories JESUS TOLD

Mary Rice Hopkins

Group | the **1** thing™